This is **ME**
MY LIFE, MY STORY,
MY TRUTH

JETAUN DALLY

This Is Me: My Life, My Story, My Truth
Copyright © 2022 by Jetaun Dally

To order additional copies of this title, or to contact the author, please e-mail: jetaunfloyd@ymail.com

First printing October 2022

Library of Congress Cataloging-in-Publication Data

Dally, Jetaun
This Is Me / by Jetaun Dally
p. cm
ISBN: 9798359429917
1. Special needs. 2. Addiction. 3. Self-Confidence.
4. Relationships. 5. Marriage. 6. Challenges. 7. Victory.

Printed in the U.S.A.

Published by AR PRESS, an American Real Publishing Company
Roger L. Brooks, Publisher
roger@incubatemedia.us
Edited by Claire Gault

14 13 12 11 10   1 2 3 4 5 6 7 8 9 10

This book is dedicated to my deceased mother, Jeanette Rose Chaney. Thank you for giving me life and showing me the do's and don'ts of motherhood. You helped to mold me into the woman I am today. I know I pushed the line a few times but because of you, I knew what lines not to cross, and for that I thank you. Rest well, we love you.

Acknowledgments

I'd like to thank my husband, kids, and family who encouraged me to follow my dreams, holding me accountable for my time and actions and loving me through the storms.

About the Author

*B*orn into a world with less than ideal circumstances, Jetaun Dally learned to be strong at a very young age.

Loyalty, love, honor, and integrity are values embodied and personified daily by Jetaun. She is a wonderful daughter, wife, mother, sister, and friend, loved by many and disliked by those who have crossed her or her family.

She is always a phone call away, a shoulder to lean on, a hand to help, and a true ride or die with a story to tell.

Table of Contents

Introduction

his book is about my life, marriage, insecurities, and addictions, as well as how I care for my special needs daughter Da'Sha Rosemarie and her siblings. It focuses on the challenges and victories I have faced over the forty-five years and counting. During this time in my life, there were some intense actions and emotions. I have not sought counseling to properly deal with all of these unresolved issues and emotions from my traumatic past. As I write this book, I am recalling and sorting through memories. I have changed the names of the characters to protect the people in my life who don't wish to be identified.

Chapter One — Jetaun

*M*y name is Jetaun, and I was born and raised in Pasadena, CA. Growing up in the "City of Roses," I was raised by my mother and grandmother. I learned how to be an independent woman, as there were few men, or should I say, *dependable* men in my life. As a child, my birth father (who I didn't know much about, besides the fact that he was a truck driver), died when I was sixteen or seventeen years old from cancer. Because I only remember meeting him a couple times, I didn't have any strong emotions when he passed. I do remember crying in the parking lot of the mortuary after seeing his body in a casket. To this day, I'm not sure if I was crying for the loss of him or just because I had never seen a dead body. I did at one point have slight contact with his daughter, my older sister, Moe, but that was as far as it went with my biological dad's side.

My mom and my biological father separated before I was born, because he used to abuse her. The man who was there in the delivery room when I was born and helped care for me, along with my mom, has been incarcerated since I was ten or eleven years old. However, before he went to jail, he took good care of me. I have pictures of me dressed in pretty dresses and diamonds, and I'm told he was very protective over me, taking me everywhere with him. He even protected me from my mother's irresponsible actions because of her drug addiction. I remember a birthday party where he rented horses to give all the kids rides. I also remember one of his side chicks coming and he quickly made her leave. My dad didn't tolerate any disrespect, especially when it came to his kids. Everybody got along: his wife and all the baby mammas. You see, my dad was a player and had multiple kids by multiple women. I only keep in touch with the kids he had with his wife, and believe it or not, to this day we are still finding out about other siblings.

I don't remember much about my life while my dad was out, and the memories I do have are vague. I remember his money-green Rolls Royce and visiting his cleaners in Altadena, California. He talks about different things and events when he calls, but I have no recollection of a lot of those days. Even after going to jail my dad still did his best to take care of his children. He would sometimes send gifts, money, or one of his girlfriends to take us shopping for school clothes and summer clothes throughout the years. This was a tremendous help to my mom as she did not always have the money to take me shopping.

At one point, my dad's side of the family took me in because my mom was not properly caring for me; it was then I went to live with my dad's mom and sister. My grandma B's house was a safe zone for me, my siblings, and cousins when our parents were living an irresponsible lifestyle with substance abuse and other issues. When my mom and dad separated, he got married. I was blessed to have a special bond with the siblings he had with his wife. His wife, whom I still call my stepmom, never treated me any different from her own children, and to this day we spend holidays and celebrate birthdays together. I love the calls from her just to check on me and my family; we all have an amazing relationship.

Once I got to my early teen years, my grandmother on my mom's side came to retrieve me from my dad's family. This was when the Idaho Street in Pasadena, California days started, and the memories began with my mom.

By then my dad had been arrested, and he was given two life sentences without possibility of parole. This left our relationship to be built over phone calls, letters, and jailhouse visits. I believe I have subconsciously blocked most of my childhood to cope. Spending a lot of time with my grandmother in her house on Idaho Street in Pasadena, I cleaned for her and took care of her at an early age. Resorting to family photo albums to recall memories has helped me to write about my childhood in this book. I have a picture of me blowing out candles on a cake that says "Happy Ninth Birthday" on it, with one of my cousins Cassie at my side. I do not remember the event, but I have the picture. I used to play with the little girl down the street, whose name was Dani. We had similar upbringings, and we looked like twins, so we called each other sisters. She lived with her dad and nana, so we played together every day in her nana's yard. I remember us getting the chicken pox together and playing school in her nana's bushes. I also remember playing with her cousins that lived around the corner from us, and a little girl named Cashea who was about a year older than me. Walking from house-to-house, us kids felt safe in our neighborhood. All our parents knew each other and were like family, so if we got out of line, each parent had permission to whoop our tails.

My grandmother had five children, four girls and one boy. There was my Aunt Jane who had done very well for herself; she went to college and married a man from England, the love of her life. Together they had one little girl, who was about two or three years older than me. Then there was my Aunt Stacy who had four or five kids, but I do not remember them all. I only grew up with two of them because the other ones lived with their dad. So, I only remember my cousin Deandre and his younger sister Fatima. Then there was my Aunt Pauly, who was a nurse. From the stories I have heard, she was the only one my dad would let babysit me when I was younger. They say he used to put $100 bills in my diaper when she watched me because she would not take his money. My Aunt Pauly had two girls who still talk about how I was so small when I spent time with them. They would put blankets in a dresser drawer and that was where I slept. My Uncle Darnell was the only son of my grandmother's kids. He was married and had four children: three boys and a girl. I spent many weekends at his house as a young girl, because his daughter and I were so close in age. We used to take all her brother's shoes out of their walk-in closet so we could set up our Barbie house. Her mom would get upset because we used her towels to make our Barbie's furniture. We were huge Barbie fans and would play in that closet for hours. Those were the good days, staying up late watching scary movies and making experimental food recipes. My grandmother's home on Idaho street in Pasadena was the only semi-stable home in my early childhood; it was where everyone would gather and come when in need. It was a safe zone, until it was not.

I remember once having to stay with my Aunt Jane and her family because my mother had gotten into an altercation with my Aunt Stacy, and my mom stabbed her five times. My aunt survived, but of course my mom went to jail. This was something that happened often, as my mom and her sister were both drug users for a long time. My Aunt Jane was the only one my mom trusted at that time and was able to care for me, so I stayed there until my mom was released from jail. They did not want to tell me what happened, but by talking to my mom on the phone I figured it out. I was used to how those jail house calls sounded from talking with my dad.

My grandmother eventually lost her home, and that is when the house hopping began. She moved at least four times before her death in November of 2010, and I will revisit that event in a later chapter.

Once my dad went to jail there were no real father figures in my life, besides all the "Uncles" my mom brought home. Because my mom suffered from substance addiction, I felt like I had to raise myself. Watching my mom with different men and getting beat and abused made me mature faster than I should have had too. There were a few that stuck around longer than others, and I considered one of them a stepdad because they were together for so long. He had three kids: two boys and a girl younger than me. He lived in Los Angeles, California. That was not the healthiest relationship either, as he was another drug dealer, and he used to really beat on her. I'd hear him hitting her in their bedroom while his kids and I sat scared, waiting for her to come out. But she would not leave him; he would just buy her gifts and say sorry, and life went on.

He took care of us kids, though. We lived in a big pretty house in Carson, California. The house had a pool and a skylight in the dining room. I shared a room with his daughter, and we painted it yellow. I hung Michael Jackson posters all over it. Of course, this man like my dad, also had money, being a drug dealer in the 80's. Thinking back now, that seems to be the type of men my mother was attracted to. I remember having big Christmases with lots of toys. My favorite and most memorable gift was a Barbie McDonald's restaurant play set he got me one Christmas. I was so happy, and

I could not wait to show my cousin who I used to play Barbies with.

My mom, as I mentioned, catered to men, so cooking and cleaning was something she did often and instilled in me. I loved her fruit salad she made us during the summer, using a scooper to cut the watermelon, cantelope, and honeydew melon into balls. I thought that was the coolest thing ever. One of my friends came over to swim one day and fell in the pool. There was a big window in the kitchen that overlooked the pool. I could just hear my mom screaming, "Get that baby, get that baby!" and one of my older stepbrothers jumping in to save her. Crazy how I remember that event but not the little girl's name. Eventually, my mom got the courage to leave her abusive relationship, and we moved back to Pasadena. The last time I saw him, he was confined to a wheelchair and relied on a caregiver for most of his needs. I always thought to myself, *Karma is real, and God do not like ugly.* All those years of abuse toward my mom and others caught up to him, I guess.

Back to Pasadena

Back in Pasadena things did not get better, and my mom still struggled with substance abuse. When I was about twelve years old, my mom attempted suicide by pill overdose. She had written a note saying who she wanted me to live with, and I found it. I chose to call the paramedics, which involved the police and led to me being taking away from my mom, and sent to a facility called Maclaren Hall for several months. The courts could not find a stable and clean place for me to go. My grandmother's home was in no condition to raise a kid so the detention center was it, until my mom could show she was fit and stable to care for me. I do not know where my uncle and aunts were or why they did not step in to care for me. That was a horrible experience to endure; that place was dirty, and the girls and staff were mean. There were fights all the time. I remember crying and begging God to get me out of there every day and night.

At one of the court hearings, I thought they were going to release me when my dad, (yes, the incarcerated one) sent his attorney to represent me. But that opened a whole other investigation when they found out who my dad was. You see, he was in jail for being a known kingpin drug dealer in the 80s and the judge did not like that at all, so I had to stay at Maclaren Hall until my mom provided documentation that he was not my biological father. It felt like forever, but they finally let me go. I can still see myself running down the hallway at full speed when they finally told me I was going home. The facility is currently facing a class action lawsuit for sexual abuse by staff members on the children that were placed there. I am so blessed and thankful to say I was never subjected to any of that kind of abuse there.

At some point we ended up back with my grandmother, and by this time she was living in a studio apartment on a steep hill down the walkway from a mental institution. This was a scary duplex with three studio units on the property. The unit in the back was occupied by a young, small-framed white man who always wore a surgical suit, mask, and gloves. I remember my mom chasing him away from our door several times and telling me never to walk to the back of the property because that man would get me, and they would never see me again. This terrified me, as a child who was left home alone most of the time and had to take the trash to the dumpster located in the back of the building. I remember running past the scary man's house like a track star, and a few times seeing him watching me from his window. The front unit was occupied by a young black man who my mom eventually started calling her brother. The reality was that they just did drugs together.

My difficult childhood growing up in a dysfunctional and unstable home setting full of substance-abusing adults showed me that I needed to break the cycle of poverty, substance abuse, and depression. I knew I needed better for myself and my future, thinking about the days we did not have food to eat. Sometimes I would have to settle for toasted bread and put a little sugar on it if I wanted something sweet. My grandmother did her best to help care for me, by making me cream of wheat for breakfast before school. I would have to go to school without lunch money and be hungry all day. My grandmother would give me a few dollars when she had it, but she was living off her social security check. My mom was stealing her money and anything of value to support her drug habit. My grandmother hid money under the mattress of her twin bed she slept on in our small studio unit. I slept on the couch and my mom she did not sleep much, as she was not home often. It was here my mom came home with news she was pregnant by one of the men who supplied her habit. I was sixteen, and I had been an only child up until then. The reality was that she did not need another kid, so there I was taking care for this little baby while my mom did whatever she was doing in the streets. She made me a mom at sixteen and I had not even had sex yet. But my sister Jasmine needed to be taken care of, so everywhere I went I had Jasmine with me; people thought she was my child.

There was always a man involved somewhere, some not as bad as others and a couple that took diligent care of us, but all of them still supplied my mom with drugs, as most of them were drug dealers. My mom and I moved around a lot, sometimes living with other people and sometimes in our own place. The Fair Oaks Apartments in Pasadena was where I had the most memories of my teenage years. We would walk to the Mexican taco truck on the corner to eat; they had the best carne asada ever. I had to be around seventeen at this time because I remember my biological father had passed away, and I received a social security check from him working as a truck driver.

I used the money to buy my first car: a white Honda Accord. Me and my play sister Stephanie used to drive it everywhere. However, I was only allowed to drive during the day because I did not even know how to drive, but most importantly, I did not have a driver's license. One night, Stephanie and I begged my mom to let us drive the car to the movies and she let us. We had no plans to go to the movies, and of course when you are doing stuff you are not supposed to be doing, something always happens. Well, I ran the back of the Honda into a pole. We made up this big lie about the car being parked at the movies and someone hitting it. We were young and dumb; my mom looked at the imprint of the pole in the bumper, laughed at us, and asked if that was the story we were sticking to. She knew very well we were lying. Of course, I lost my driving privileges that night, but my mom was not mad; her and her friends laughed at us for trying to lie about what happened. After that night I was only allowed to drive back and forth to school and that was it.

My mom and I knew a lot of people in our apartment complex. My mom's friends had kids around my age, so I would bounce from apartment to apartment hanging out with the other kids in the building. In these apartments my mom was dealing with another abusive man who she did drugs with. One day, I could hear him in the room beating on my mom. Well, I was not a kid anymore, and I was not going to sit and wait for her to come out. I ran in the room and started hitting this grown man in the head, yelling, "Get off my momma." I guess me coming in gave my mom the courage to fight back, because now we were both hitting this man until he ran out the house and down the stairs of the building. We were hot on his tail. That was the end of that relationship, thank God. You see, no matter what my mom did or how many times she disappointed me, she was still my mom, and I was going to protect her and my little sister Jasmine in any way I could.

Chapter Two — Da'Sha Rosemarie

A couple of years later I met a boy nicknamed "D-Mack" by his fellow gang-friends. He was about the same age as I was but yes, a boy, because he never acted like a real man even to this day; you will hear about that later in this book. I got in relationship with D-Mack and was taught early on to cater to him and his needs by my mother. At this time my mother, Jasmine and I were living in a one-bedroom apartment. I can remember her saying things like, "Get up and cook that man something to eat" at eighteen years old. Living in a one-bedroom apartment, my mother allowed D-Mack to spend the night. We were allowed to share a bed in the bedroom because she was occupied with her friends and substance abuse in the front room, going in and out of the house. Needless to say, I was pregnant by the age of nineteen years old. I was devastated, thinking my mom was going to be so mad when she found out. But my mother was actually happy, and looking back, sometimes I feel like she planned it.

I had a hard pregnancy; living a rough and stressful life, I did not gain much weight during the nine months carrying my child. I have always been a small person.

When I was pregnant at nineteen years old, I was five feet tall and 104 pounds, and by the time I gave birth, I only weighed 114 pounds. When I went to the doctor, the nurse and doctors said, "She's so small" while performing the ultrasound. At one visit the doctor changed my due date, extending it a month because of the size of my stomach, not by my last period. This being my first pregnancy, I trusted the doctor knew what he was doing. At a later visit I was told that my daughter's heart rate was irregular, and I should go home and rest, and a specialist would reach out to me. I caught the city bus to all my doctors' appointments; I did not have a car and neither did my mother or the baby's father. When I got home, I did not feel good about the doctor's advice to wait on a specialist to call me. I told my mom I was going to go to the hospital, and I was going to tell them I was having pain so they would give me a full checkup, and that is what I did. Once I got to Huntington Hospital in Pasadena, they hooked me up to all their monitors and they confirmed my daughter's heart rate was irregular, low in fact. They also confirmed that I had no fluids in my bag and that my daughter was in distress, and at that time they scheduled me for an emergency C-section. Two hours later, Da'Sha Rosemarie was born. She weighed two pounds, five ounces, and was nineteen inches long. I could literally hold her in the palm of my hand, she was so small.

The doctors soon gathered me and her father in a conference room and explain to us that our daughter was born with a virus called CMV, or Cytomegalovirus, which we now know causes stunted growth, seizures, and brain damage. Then they told us that they did not expect her to survive past the age of five years old. I was devastated, young, and did not know what to do. My mother immediately called an attorney. Before I was discharged from the hospital, there was a lawyer at my bedside ready to sue the OBGYN who took care of me and misdiagnosed me while I was pregnant. Da'Sha stayed in the hospital for four months, and during this time I remained at my grandmother's house and caught the bus to the hospital every day to hold my baby. Because Da'Sha was in the Neonatal Intensive Care Unit (NICU), there was a strict sterile process everyone had to go through to see her. The sterilization process was what doctors and nurses go through when they are about to operate on a patient. First, I had to put on a sterile gown that tied in the back. Then, I had to scrub my hands and arms up to my elbows with a packaged, sterile scrub brush, making sure I scrubbed good under my fingernails. Once I was done scrubbing, I had to put on those blue surgical gloves and a mask. Then I could go in.

Da'Sha had jaundice so she was in an incubator, and her skin was a yellowish color. She had a small tube going down her nose for feedings and wires attached to her tiny body to monitor her heart rate, blood pressure, and breathing. The first few weeks were the hardest because they would not let me hold her. I could just stick my hands through the two holes and rub her hands to let her know mommy was there and I loved her. Her father and I were the only ones who were allowed to visit her in NICU. After a while, the nurse got the "okay" to allow us to hold Da'Sha. She was almost a month old the first time I got to hold my baby girl, and all I could do was cry. She was so small, with tubes and wires attached to her. I had to be very careful, and I sat in a rocking chair next to the incubator and rocked her for hours a day, not knowing what God had in store for our future, but I knew I was not going to leave her side. My godsister Dani was able to go in and see Da'Sha while she was in NICU once when I was not there. I'm thinking, *they just did not realize it was not me or what?* but I was happy she got to see her. You see, Da'Sha was born on Dani's birthday, so she always thanks me for that special birthday gift, even to this day.

Four months later Da'Sha was released from the hospital, weighing a little over five pounds. I took her home with me to my grandmothers to care for her. By then my grandmother lived in South Pasadena in a one-bedroom apartment. My mom was not around much, and I don't recall where she and Jasmine were at during this time, and my grandmother was in and out of the hospital. So, for the short time we stayed there it was just me and Da'Sha.

Soon Da'Sha's father and I moved into our own apartment on Summit Street in Pasadena, right next door to his mom's apartment. When I say, "Right next door," I mean that if my door was open too much it would block her door from opening: we were that close. This was where the physical abuse started. Da'Sha's dad was an alcoholic and when he got drunk, he would not only physically assault me, but also force me to have sexual intercourse against my will. Feeling stuck in this relationship with my child's father, I continued to stay and endure the emotional and physical abuse. One day I had an intense pain in my abdomen, and the pain got so bad that it brought me to tears. I do not know where my mom was at this time, because I called my Aunt Pauly to take me to the hospital. It was there I found out D-Mack had given me an STD. It made sense because D-Mack never hid the fact he slept around with multiple women. It seemed like he was proud to be a male whore and taking advantage of women and using them to get whatever he wanted.

One night after a night of drinking I walked in on him having sexual relations with a thirteen-year-old girl he claimed to be his play-sister. Later, they conceived two children together before she was even sixteen years old. I was so young, confused on what to do, and scared of being alone to take care of this child with special needs, so I stayed in our toxic relationship. We were financially unstable and eventually lost our apartment. Now homeless, we had to stay with multiple friends and family until we decided to move to Palmdale with his father's side of the family. We wanted a better future out of Pasadena and the traumatic events that had taken place. We stayed with this father and stepmother for a few months before getting our own apartment. We were so excited to get out of his dad's house, at least, I know I was.

Things were fine for a while. I started working for a cleaning company called White Gloves while Da'Sha's dad stayed home to care for her. I know, kind of backwards huh, the man should be working while the woman takes care of homelife. He did do odd-and-end construction jobs here and there but nothing stable or permanent, so I had to do what was necessary to pay the bills. Things were looking good the first year, and then one day the seizures started. I did not know what was going on; my baby was twitching, and I did not know what to do. I called the ambulance, and we ended up in the hospital for a few days. They told me that yes, it was part of CMV, and prescribed her Phenobarbital to help keep them under control. This was the beginning of our hospital stays. I decided I needed to be at home to care for my baby, so I quit the cleaning job. Luckily, I did, because a few months later Da'Sha started throwing up and choking on her food. One day she turned blue and stopped breathing. I thought to myself, *this is it, we did not even make it to five years old.* Thank God we got to the hospital in time, and they brought my baby back to life. That would be the first time she stopped breathing on me.

We found out that she was aspirating fluids and they would need to put a G-tube in her stomach so that we could feed her, and she could no longer have any liquids by mouth. Scared to death, I had to learn how to insert the feeding extension, and thread it through the feeding pump for a continuous flow through the night. Thinking to myself, *Am I going to be able to do this is this going to be forever?* I had so many thoughts and emotions going on, but I knew I had to do whatever it took because she was my child, and I was going to love and care for her with all I had.

I needed to make some changes in my life for the better of my daughter, so my first step was getting rid of the father. He was abusive and a drunk, and I did not want him around me and my child. He was causing more stress and pain then good, and not to mention two babies while we were together with a minor. I was just over the abuse, and to this day the smell of beer makes me sick to my stomach.

Chapter Three — Palmdale Days

*n*ow I was a single mom living on my own, and I needed a new job. There was a local gas station across the street from the apartments I lived in, so I applied for a position at the pizza parlor that was in the back of the gas station called Piccadilly Pizzas. I got the job, and the manager there loved me. He was confident enough in me that I opened in the morning and ran the place by myself in the afternoon. I made arrangement for my little sister Alexus on my dad's side (yes, the incarcerated one) to watch Da'Sha while I worked. Once again, things were going okay until the pizza place and the Social Security check didn't cover the bills. Now, Da'Sha and I had to move to a cheaper apartment, not far from the first apartment but definitely not as nice. The upside was it was the same building my siblings lived in, so it did help as far as helping me with Da'Sha so I could continue to work and manage the bills.

It was at Piccadilly Pizza that I met Donald and all of his friends. Donald and his friends would come over my little townhome and hang out often, turning my home into the hang-out. Looking back, it was not the most responsible time in my life; there was a lot of late-night functions and drinking during this time. I was lonely and enjoyed the company. Donald's friends started calling me "sis" and would help me from time to time, buying food and things they saw I need in the house. To be honest, I did need the assistance as a single mom, as Da'Sha's dad did absolutely nothing to help with the care of her once we separated. It didn't take long for Donald and me to develop a romantic relationship. However, he was what they call a player. He was still involved with his son's mother Harper and several other women that caused a lot of problems for us. Harper would ride up and down my street looking for him and me, and when we saw each other, the fights were on. We had multiple run-ins fighting over this man who couldn't leave either one of us alone. I made some irresponsible decisions during this time in my life. None ever subjected Da'Sha to harm, but still did us no good either.

Da'Sha eventually started having more seizures and required tube feedings, breathing treatments, and physical therapy to help with her motor skills. It was obvious again that it was time to make some changes. I was still going back and forth with the attorneys about the malpractice lawsuit, and really needed the money to take care of me and Da'Sha and move us out of the ghetto environment we were living in. Other than the support of my siblings and a few cousins that hung around from Da'Sha's dad side of the family, I didn't know many people in Palmdale. One of my close friends Lynn, and her then three-year-old daughter soon moved to Palmdale as well and was able to get an apartment in the same building as me. This was very helpful to me, as were both single moms and able to help each other physically and emotionally. I remember us catching the bus to the grocery store and catching a cab back home with all of our groceries. Just splitting the cab fare helped us both out financially. Most of the time, we would cook one meal and eat at each other's house. Lynn and I made the best out of our situation living as single moms. We shared long nights playing cards and caring for our girlswho were just a month apart, but since Da'Sha suffered from development disorders, Lynn's daughter and mine did not function on the same level. I remember I used to buy her daughter all the toys I would have brought for Da'Sha if she could play with them: doll houses, play kitchens, and other toys little girls play with at age three and four. At that time, Da'Sha was the size of a six-month-old, still playing with toy rattles and plush dolls. It was here Lynn met and fell in love with her now husband of fifteen years, Will. We became one family and now call one another sisters, knowing each other for over twenty-six years now.

Chapter Four — The Trust Fund

In 1999, the malpractice lawsuit against the OBGYN that cared for me while I was pregnant was finally settled. The doctor lost his medical license due to other women who had come forward with malpractice cases against him. By then Da'Sha was four years old, and I was twenty-three years old and struggling to survive financially. The lawyers appointed a trustee to handle the special needs trust fund that had been established for Da'Sha and Da'Sha only. You see, the judge had decided that I was not affected by the disabilities my child was born with. However, the judge did agree the doctor was at fault for not paying enough attention to me during my pregnancy. It actually came out during the depositions that the doctor was having personal issues and it was distracting him from his job. I didn't understand what they meant by I was not affected by this, like who was taking care of Da'Sha, taking her to the doctor's, and staying at the hospital all those nights with her? I was doing the G-tube feeding and giving her the medications prescribed by the doctors. So, how was my life not affected by my child's disabilities? But again, I was young and dumb and needed the money, so I accepted what they decided for me and signed the papers.

The trustee was an older white woman with a head full of gray hair. I didn't know how this relationship was going to play out, but the trustee drove up to Palmdale from Pasadena and we immediately started looking for a home for Da'Sha and I to live in. After couple months of looking with an awesome realtor named Patricia, we found a nice three-bedroom home with a pool; it was beautiful. I remember the trustee taking Patricia, myself, and Lynn to lunch to sign all the papers, and I was so happy. After lunch I expressed the need for a vehicle to transport Da'Sha to doctor appointments and such, and the same day she took us to the Nissan dealership and purchased a Nissan Pathfinder. Da'Sha and I now had a beautiful home in a nice neighborhood and a reliable car. The trustee started to pay me as a caregiver, and I used the money to furnish our new home. Then the money ran out and the trust was no longer able to pay me as a caregiver. She told me that the trust couldn't afford certain things anymore. I recall asking the trustee to purchase a desktop for the home to help with research and things for Da'Sha, and she agreed. However, she wanted her computer guy to find the right computer and they would purchase it, which I thought was weird because how would he know what I was looking for? Then I got the first accountant for the year of the trust, and I saw the trustee paid the computer guy for his services. I was upset and couldn't understand why she had to pay someone else to do something I was capable of doing myself. That was when I started to realize how the trust worked. This didn't sit well with me, and I expressed my frustration to the trustee, along with how difficult it was to take care of Da'Sha without having to worry about her money being mishandled. Her response to me was to think about putting Da'Sha in a living facility. I was furious at her, yelling at her "This was my child," and I would never send her to a home to rot away. I have never liked facilities; I feel the people there do not love or care for the residents who reside there. They only take their money, and in a lot of cases, the residents are abused physically and sexually. That was never going to be an option for my child. Needless to say, the trustee never mentioned that again.

Now that Da'Sha and I are older, I can see how I got screwed in the settlement. The settlement was for roughly $475,000 but the trust was only issued $157,000, so the lawyers walked away with 300,000, as if they were the ones who suffered from the malpractice and now had to raise a disabled child. Here we are later, and the trust is binding and broke, and I am told that if something ever happens to Da'Sha, the assets (meaning the house I have raised my children in for the last nineteen years) will be sold to pay back the state for caring for Da'Sha all these years. So, I would not only suffer the loss of my child but also the loss of our family home. This seemed so unfair but what could I do? I signed the papers not knowing any better or having the proper representation.

Chapter Five — On To Better Things In Palmdale

n 2001, Da'Sha and I enjoyed our new home and stable environment. By then, my little sister Jasmine had moved in because my mom was struggling to care for her. So, I stepped up taking custody of my then six- or seven-year-old little sister and things were good. We had a routine; the girls had their own rooms and were both in school.

Da'Sha started going to school and physical therapy, and she really seemed to be doing well. The school system in Palmdale, specifically Buena Vista School, was terrific. Transportation provided door-to-door service, so the school bus picked her up every morning and dropped her off every afternoon right in front of our house. The teacher at Buena Vista were super nice and loving; they communicated with me daily about Da 'Sha's day through a journal that we kept in her backpack. They would tell me about her day, and I could tell them about any issues or concerns I had, so we were always on the same page. I was invited to the school whenever I wanted to see Da'Sha or just pop in to see what activities they were working on with her. The teacher loved Da'Sha and Da'Sha showed her love for them as well. This gave me so much comfort, as I did not let Da'Sha out of my sight often. I was her sole care provider and very protective over her. I still have the arts and crafts they would send home, and the personal gifts they helped her make me on holidays such as Mother's Day and Christmas. It was things like that that a mother with a disabled child really appreciated, because Da'Sha could not do it on her own. Being my only child at the time, those special gifts made my day. This was by far the best school Da'Sha has ever been to, as I will explain in a later chapter.

Da'Sha was also a part of California Children's Services, also known as CCS. This program provided physical and speech therapy to Da'Sha. That is where I believe Da'Sha learned to say "Mama" and "Hi Da'Sha," as that was what she heard the most of. Physical therapy was trying to work with Da 'Sha's motor skills, attempting to teach her how to hold things in her hand and walk. CCS provided a personalized wheelchair for Da'Sha, along with leg AFO (braces) and gloves sized to fit her hands, as she tends to bite herself when frustrated; she still does that to this day. The Regional Center did not provide much more or less; they just stayed connected with us to ensure we had everything we needed, and if we did not get it from CCS, they would do their best to provide what was needed. They liked to give papers on different support groups for families with special needs children. However, I never took advantage of those groups as I had my own personal support group, which included my best friend Lynn and my siblings from my dad's side who all lived in Palmdale not far from us.

I really needed my support system when Da'Sha, a cousin of mine, and I were in a bad car accident. It was in a residential neighborhood in front of the school Jasmine attended at the time. We were leaving our home and had not gone but a block away when a man ran a stop sign and hit the back axle of my Pathfinder. That caused us to flip over on the hood of the SUV and we slid halfway down the street. We were all hanging upside down in the SUV. Pedestrians that heard the crash came out their homes to help. I was able to get myself out and went to get Da'Sha, out who was all smiles because she enjoyed hanging upside down. When I went to unbuckle her car seat, I couldn't feel my arm. A stranger came up and said, "Look at your arm, let me help you." When I looked at my arm it was covered in blood. I guess when we flipped over, I held my hand up so when my window shattered the glass, it cut my arm. We all had to go to the hospital, but I was the only one injured. My cousin and Da'Sha were fine. My arm looked like ground beef; I could see the glass and pavement sticking out of it. I had to have surgery on my arm to have the glass removed, and the pain at night was excruciating. I went through a couple of months of therapy to recover. I was thankful for my family who banded together to not only help with caring for Da'Sha, but helped keep my house clean and drove us to all our appointments. That accident left me with a large ugly scar on the back of my forearm. To this day I can still feel sharp pain when it gets cold.

I was still in an on and off again relationship with Donald but since he could not commit to me, I could not commit to him. Although he was coming over every day and almost every night, things were still not right with us, because he was still playing games by having relations with Harper and other women.

I started going to visit another best friend I grew up with in Pasadena. We shall call her "Stephanie." Stephanie and I used to run together when I was younger and never lost contact. I consider her my sister too; I've known her since I was fourteen years old. We went to middle school together and everyone thought we were sisters, so we rolled with it. We both got pregnant with our first and last child both a month apart.

One day I went to visit her and met a guy named Elijah. I thought he was so cute: he was short with a bald head. Well, we eventually hooked up and started a relationship, at least, that is what I thought it was. I knew things were off with how secretive he was, but I did not pay much attention to it as I had a lot going on with taking care of my two girls. I broke off the relationship with Donald when Elijah started coming to my home in Palmdale. He would stay a few days then leave for a couple of weeks. Of course, I got pregnant, and he was not happy about it. I remember him saying it was not a good time for him to have another kid, as he had two girls from a prior relationship. But I was happy and had wanted the chance to have a normal baby in my eyes without disabilities, so I told him that with or without you, this baby was coming.

When I was about seven months pregnant, Da'Sha had a major seizure and would not stop vomiting, so we rushed her to the hospital in Lancaster. This hospital had the worst service and was the only close hospital in the area at the time. Da'Sha was seizing for three hours and constantly throwing up. I remember Lynn and I finding towels and changing sheets while the doctors and nurses did nothing. When I requested to have Da'Sha transferred to Loma Linda Children's Hospital in Los Angeles, they agreed, however transportation took forever so I told them I would take my child myself. The nurse called security on me and told me if I attempted to remove Da'Sha, she would have me arrested and call Child Protective Services on me. I was furious and crying, watching my child seizing and vomiting while they did nothing to help her. Eventually the ambulance arrived to transport her, and they took her to Loma Linda. The next day when I was leaving my house on my way to the hospital, Child Protective Services were walking up my driveway. Once again, I got upset about the situation and lack of care from the Lancaster hospital and explained what happened. The social workers agreed with me and understood why I wanted to take my child somewhere else and close the complaint the hospital filed on me. Da'Sha had to stay in the hospital for a few days, and to this day we don't understand why or how she was vomiting the way she was. The doctors claimed they had tied off her esophagus so that she was not supposed to be able to vomit because it could cause her to aspirate.

Apparently, the doctor who performed the procedure for her g-tube button placement didn't do something right. That night my baby threw up for hours.

A few weeks later while Elijah was visiting, I put his clothes I had washed back in his duffle bag and found a second phone. That was when I knew something was not right with this man; he was obviously living a double life. Back then we did not text, so there was nothing for me to go through. I started asking questions and eventually found out I was not the only woman in his life. In fact, I was the side chick. He had a whole other woman, and she was pregnant too. *Wow*, I thought to myself, *this explains a lot.*

Valentine's Day approached, and I could not get ahold of Elijah, so I called my friend Stephanie to see what she knew; Stephanie knew a lot of people and always knew the business of others. She then informed me that the other woman was in labor, and he was probably at the hospital with her. There I was, seven months pregnant on Valentine's Day alone, and my child's father was at the hospital having a baby with another woman. Upset by this news, I reached out to my on and off again flame Donald, who of course came running. I know it sounds bad, but the love Donald and I had for one another surpassed all the issues we put each other through. He came over and held me all night that night, and honestly, it felt good. He did not care that I was pregnant by another man, because he had just had another baby with his baby mamma Harper, so in our weird world we were even. But all things must come to an end. Like Betty Wright said in her song "As We Lay," it's morning, and now it's time for us to say goodbye. Donald left, and Elijah eventually showed up with his excuses. Bothered by the situation but not wanting to cause stress to my unborn child, I let it go.

A couple months later, our son was on his way. I had gone to one of my stress test appointments and they were concerned my son's heart rate was a little elevated. They didn't want to take any chances because of my history, so they decided to take him out. So now I was about to have another C-section. We were not completely ready. Lynn and I were at the hospital still figuring out his name while we waited on the doctor and Elijah to get prepared for the delivery. Safe and healthy, I now had a handsome baby boy we call Ace, like on a deck of cards, because he was both of our first boy. I was still not sure what I was doing with this guy, but wanting my son to have a father I let him convince me to move out of Palmdale in search for a larger home so our son could also have his own room, and we could have a fresh start. And my dumb ass did it. Lynn and I searched all over looking for a new house and settled for a four-bedroom home in Adelanto, California, forty-five minutes away from Palmdale in the middle of nowhere. I don't know what I was thinking letting this man talk me into moving away from my beautiful home with a pool and all my family, but that is exactly what we did.

Chapter Six — The Move To Adelanto

*I*n July of 2003, my son Ace was only a month old when we were just about to close escrow on our new house. I told the realtor we needed to clean before I moved in, so she gave us the keys. Lynn, Will, Elijah and I went in and not only cleaned the house but painted every room. My son's room was sky blue with red helicopters and airplanes on the wall. Jasmine's room was purple and Da'Sha's room was a bright canary yellow. It kind of felt good, like a fresh start. I needed to get away from Donald and that Harper drama, and I thought I could start a family with Elijah. By this time, my mom had moved in with me as well. She was doing better and off the hard drugs, so she was supposed to help with the kids. This gave me the opportunity to start working again.

I started working at Arco gas station not even ten minutes from my house, which was convenient for me to come home for lunch and check on the kids. Elijah of course had started his disappearing act again, coming and going. He would call and tell me where to pick him up from, never a real address, just outside an apartment building or other random location. In the back of my mind, I always felt like I was picking him up and dropping him off to the next woman. He would usually stay for a week or so and leave for two weeks somewhere else. This was not working for me, because I was getting older and smarter, not taking the situation lightly anymore. Our son was a little over a year old when we got into a physical altercation, and I told him it was over between us. I think we both knew a long time ago, so we did not go back and forth about it, we just ended things.

I was single again, with two kids and working at a gas station in a town in which I knew nobody. My family was either in Palmdale or Pasadena, and Lynn and her family had moved to Arizona. Now I was relying on my mom to help me with the kids so I could continue to work and pay my bills. I have a picture of me with Da'Sha sitting next to me and Ace in my lap, and I was reading them a book. I was still in my work uniform and hair was a mess, but mommy duties called: tired or not.

This went on for a while, until one day I got a call from Donald. We started communicating again over the phone, then I started making trips to see him in Palmdale. It was like we never separated. The love was still there and strong as ever. I don't know what it was about that man, but we had a bond and chemistry that would not die.

I remember the first time Elijah came to see Ace, and Donald was leaving my house. Elijah was so upset that he was ready to fight. He said he didn't want another man around his son. I laughed so hard, telling him I had never approached any of his other women and we were over, so he needed to accept that there was going to be another man in my life and around his son. The way I saw it was if he did not want another man around his son, he would have been a better man to me. Why did he think I was going to stay single because I had a kid with him? That was not going to happen.

Donald and his son Jr. moved in about a year later, and we were doing well. I had to stop working at the gas station because Da'Sha had a seizure one day, and I had to take her to the hospital. I let my boss know my daughter had a seizure, and I did not know if I was going to make it in that day or not. That man called me every hour asking me when I was coming in. Da'Sha did not have to stay in the hospital that time, but I was so upset at all the calls from my manager that when I left the hospital, I went straight to Arco and told him that I quit. I could not understand why he would stress me out even more then I was while at the hospital with my child. That was the last job I had. I knew then I could never work for anyone else because my children's health and well-being would always be put first.

I was officially a stay-at-home mom, and Jasmine was attending a local school in the area. However, the schools for disabled children were not as attentive or supportive as the school in Palmdale. Da'sha transferred to quite a few different schools in the area. There was one school in Adelanto Da'sha attended for a very short time. Da'sha used to fuss every day when it was time to get on the school bus. This was out of Da'Sha's normal, happy behavior, so I started do pop-up visits at the school. They were unorganized and had kids walking around without supervision. It was this school I noticed Da'sha coming home with bruises. I immediately made a police report and removed Da'sha from the school. Da'Sha did not attend another school for a long time after that, as we were both traumatized. Eventually, with the pressure from the school district, I found another school for Da'sha to attend. This school was more structured and had total control of the classroom. The teacher and teacher aides were very understanding to my concerns and all of Da'sha's needs. Da'sha attended that school until she maxed out the program because of her age.

Maxing out of programs has been the biggest issue for us in a lot of the programs for disabled kids. Da'sha may be over the age of eighteen, however she is wheelchair bound, still in diapers, G-tube fed, and has the mental functions of a six-month-old. So, stopping her physical and speech therapy because she is not progressing to their standards or because of her age was something I never understood. This left Da'sha at home with me twenty-four hours a day, seven days a week. I became her therapist. I did a range of motion exercises and talked to her, trying to teach her sounds, and none of this I had a degree in or certificate to teach. I feel like they should have more programs for people with disabilities who are over the age of eighteen years old. It was as if they thought she was going to outgrow her disabilities or something. Home life was complicated but good. Donald never had a real job: he sold drugs. There I was following in my mother's footsteps, attracted to the same kind of men I always said I would stay away from. Donald wasn't a big drug dealer like my dad or anything close so he could not afford to pay all the bills and other financial matters, but he did give me money for groceries, and he liked to dress nice, so he brought all our clothes and shoes. He came home with jewelry, bottles of perfume, and other things that his clients would sell him. I know doesn't sound like much, but it was more than anyone else had done, so I appreciated it.

This went on for years. I would be at home with not only my kids but his two kids as well. Yes, eventually Harper and I ended our feud, and I let their second child come over on weekends. Donald was still running the streets, not necessarily cheating, but just not home as much as I needed or wanted him to be. This caused us to separate again for about six months. During those six months I started meeting people in my area and hanging out with them, but not dating or seeing anyone left the door open for Donald to step right back in. Once again, it took one phone call; here we go again. That time around I got pregnant. It was in September, and Harper and I went to a restaurant for her birthday. I ordered a margarita and could not drink it, because the smell of the drink made my stomach turn. I came home and Stephanie brought a pregnancy test to my house. It was positive. I remember her saying, "Better you then me." Funny thing was, she was also pregnant at that time and just didn't know yet.

I couldn't believe after ten years of dealing with Donald on and off we were finally about to have a baby. We were both so happy, and he started changing his lifestyle for the better for our family. He even proposed and bought me a ring. We finally got it together and were expanding our family.

November came around and Donald, the kids, and I went to his mom's house for Thanksgiving. I remember him gathering the last few things he had at his mom's house and loading the suburban truck up to take it back to our house. Jr. wanted to stay with his grandma for a few days, as she had two younger boys close to his age.

A couple of days later Da'Sha had a therapy appointment to go to, so Donald took us to that appointment, and then we got something to eat. Later, he dropped us off at home so he could go to Palmdale to take care of some things. The day turned to night, so I called him to see where he was, and he said he was stopping to get us a few movies to watch, and he would be on his way. I must have fallen asleep waiting, because I woke up and it was 12a.m.; I could hear an ambulance in the distance. Wondering why he was not home, I called him and got no answer. I called again and again and again: still nothing. By then, I was convinced he was up to his old ways again. So, I left him an ugly voicemail telling him he better be dead or in jail, I was so upset. I paced the floors for hours looking out the front window and sitting outside waiting, mad as hell. Three, then four hours passed, and then I was panicking. The phone finally rang, and it was his mom. She was hysterical, saying she got a phone call from the police who told her that Donald was in an accident, but she could not talk to them, so she told them to call me.

A few minutes later, the phone rang again: it was the highway patrol. The officer confirmed what type of vehicle he was driving because it was registered to me, and then proceeded to tell me he had been in an accident. By then I was throwing some clothes on and asked what hospital they were taking him to. The female officer's exact words were, "He's not going to the hospital, he's going to the morgue." I screamed and dropped to my knees. We later found out he fell asleep driving home on a two-way highway and swerved into oncoming traffic. He was hit head on by a semi-truck and died instantly from blunt force trauma. He was only about fifteen minutes from the house. I realized the ambulance I had heard in the distance was probably going to him.

Because he was in my truck, I had no way to get anywhere so Harper came to get me, and we drove to his mom's house. Everyone was devastated and crying; we could have never imagined this would have happened. I stayed at his mom's house for a few days to help in any way I could. Donald's sister asked me to help with making arrangements because she said she couldn't do it alone, and her mom was in no state to make any decisions. I remember taking calls from the mortuary, asking what we wanted them to do with his clothes and belongings. They also asked if he was an organ donor, and other things they needed to know. There I was trying to be as strong as I could for his mother, sister, and kids, but inside I was dying. I thought to myself, *I was three months pregnant, and he was never going to meet our baby.* It was hard to prepare for the funeral service, pick out clothes for him to wear, and decide which cemetery to lay him to rest at. But the hardest part was picking out his casket, and that broke me; I couldn't hold it together any longer. I broke down. The funeral service was huge; there were so many people who showed up to give condolences and to show their love and support: my family included. Donald was loved and respected. I remember Lynn holding me while I sat and cried, saying he looked like he was sleeping. That memory is embedded in my mind. I still have the newspaper article about the crash in my Bible.

Chapter Seven — The Aftermath

*A*fter the service, things started getting uneasy between Donald's family and I. They weren't sure my baby was his because we had just got back together after being separated, and they started treating me funny. They wanted all his clothes, shoes, and any belongings he had at my house. Even Harper started spreading rumors and telling people lies. Once again, I hated Harper, wanting to fight her pregnant and all. As if I was not grieving enough, I didn't have a car to get Da'Sha or myself to our appointments. Because my suburban truck was completely totaled in the accident, I had to figure so many things out. I was now a single mom of a special needs child, Ace was five, and I was about to have another baby. Lord have mercy on me.

My mom stayed around for a bit, but I believe Donald's death affected her too because she started using drugs again. Running back and forth to Pasadena, she left me on my own. Thank God Jasmine was now old enough to help around the house and helped with the kids, but she still had school and I didn't want to put too much on her. I had the support system of Lynn, Stephanie, and a few others who would call and check on me. One of my cousins Cassie from the birthday picture at my grandmother's house came up to visit me. I remember her taking me to Olive Garden for lunch and we talked for hours. But it was the nights I was alone that I wept the most. The thoughts, memories, and ugly voicemail I left haunted me. I was depressed and sinking fast. So, I turned to God. I started reading my Bible every day and night, and I started talking to God more and more every day. The books of Psalms and Proverbs really got me through my darkest moments while grieving the loss of my fiancé and being pregnant with our child. By this time Lynn and her family had moved to Arizona, so I started making trips to see them out there.

On one of my visits, Lynn threw me a surprise baby shower. Her and her husband's family came together and brought me all kinds of gifts for the baby, which we then knew was a girl. I thought, *How am I going to get all this stuff back to California?* Then when I came back to California, Stephanie threw me another baby shower. By then she was almost nine months pregnant herself. Remember her joking, "Better you then me" when I took that pregnancy test? We later found out she was already six weeks pregnant and didn't know. So, here we were having my second baby shower and we both had big bellies; I still laugh at those pictures from the baby shower. Now it was getting closer to my delivery date but also my son's birthday. I remember telling my pregnant belly, "You stay in there until after your brother's birthday party," and she did.

Four days after the party, she was on her way. Of course, because I had a C- section with my other two kids the doctor did not want to take any chances, so as soon as I had the slightest contraction, he scheduled the procedure. I also decided to get my tubes tied at the same time. Against everyone's advice I did not care; I was over love, and I didn't want to have to raise any more children on my own. I called Stephanie and told her it was time, so she was there in the delivery room with me in place of Donald so I would not be alone. A few hours later I had a healthy beautiful baby girl; we will call her "Jenny." Donald's sister and mom came to see me, and couldn't believe how much she looked like him. They could not deny that was his baby for sure: she was literally his twin. His sister, not having any kids at that time, fell in love with her. By the time I was released from the hospital, Lynn and her family were on their way from Arizona. By then Lynn was married with four kids of her own, and her mom was coming too. Her mom had always treated me like a daughter, so she was excited to see her new granddaughter. I have a small but strong support system that show up and show out every time I need them.

Once Jenny was old enough for my mom to watch, I started going out to clubs and events. Believe it or not, I started hanging out with Harper again. I know we had a complicated on-and-off-again relationship, and we still do to this day. But after being pregnant and still dealing with the death of Donald, I spiraled out of control. Harper was like my demon-side personality. No cares, no kids, just a good time. Sometimes I stayed away from my house and kids for the whole weekend, going to clubs, drinking, and smoking marijuana. One night I almost had a threesome. Harper, who was openly bisexual, stepped in and said, "No, she's not that type of woman and will regret it later." And for that I was thankful she had my back in that situation. Yes, I was out of control and almost lost myself completely. Grief will have you doing thing out of your normal character, and I started realizing I needed to get my head and feelings in order.

After that I slowed down on my trip to Palmdale to hang out. But one day I ran into a girl I knew from Pasadena named Tay; she was one of D-Mack's cousins. She used to live with his mom when we lived on Summit Street in Pasadena. I hadn't seen her in years but when I ran into her, she was staying with some friends around the corner from my house and invited me over. After going over to hang out a few times, I found out the girl's boyfriend did tattoos out of the house, so there was some traffic and people hanging out drinking and smoking. It looked like I just found a closer spot to home to hang out, while my mom was home with my kids. The tables had turned, and it was now her turn to be a mom and grandmom to my kids. While this probably was no better than hanging out in Palmdale, I felt better that I was home every night with my kids and close enough that if Da'Sha had a seizure I could get to her quickly.

One day while I was hanging out with Tay, I ran into a familiar face. It was a young guy I met when I worked at the Arco gas station named Ricky. We had exchanged numbers back then, but after talking over the phone I realized he was too young and immature for me at that time. I also saw he had a girlfriend when they came in the Arco together one day. So, this deterred me from him. By then it had been a year since Donald passed and I was looking for some male attention, so I gave him my number. I did not hear from him right away, but one day about two weeks later, Tay called and said this guy was over there asking about me and wanted me to come over to hang out, and so I did.

Again, not looking for anything more than sex from this young man, we started hanging out. I would go to his apartment he lived in at night, have relations, and return home before my kids could even miss me. At this time, I had a childhood friend who was having a hard time living with me. It was her and her three kids, who were all older than mine, so she was helping Jasmine with mine while I was spending time with Rickey. Wow, I'm sounding more and more like my mom by the page.

Eventually I started feeling some type of way about leaving my house at night creeping with this very young man, so I told him I couldn't come over at night anymore. Well, he didn't like that, so he started coming to visit me. Once my friend and her kids moved out, he started coming over even more. He definitely had my attention, pulling up to my house on a dirt bike with no helmet on. He had a long ponytail and was very in shape back then, but again, he was so young. Then he started bringing his son Camron with him. Next thing I knew, it was becoming an every day and night thing. His son was only two years old then, and he was raising him on his own. His child's mother and him had separated shortly before we met and was not in the picture, but would occasionally get Camron on weekends. We started spending so much time together that Camron started calling me "Mom" because that was what he heard my kids calling me. This was not something I wanted, so I told my kids to call me "Taun" around him so he wouldn't call me mom. This was out of respect for his mom that I had not even met yet. Taun was a nickname I had as a child that my family still called me by.

This little sex fling was starting to look more like a relationship that neither one of us would admit to. I recall meeting his mom Patty one day when we picked her up from the airport. She asked me what I wanted with her son. You see, this young man was ten years younger than me, and he and I were trying to figure out what we were doing together. I told her we were just friends hanging out, as we had been telling everyone else. I had now met most of his close friends and his sisters, and they all said we were not acting like we were just friends. I met his brother Jim, who was in the military, and he and his family were relocating to North Carolina. Ricky had to drive him and his wife Nadine to the airport early the next morning, so we spent the night at his sisters' house. Ricky and I slept on the couch together when his brother came in and said, "I ain't never slept on the couch like that with my friend." We laughed and stuck to our story of just being friends with benefits. This went on for several months of us being in denial about our relationship.

One day Ricky got a phone call from his mom, who said his little sister Chloe, living in Arizona at the time, had some sort of medical issue and they could not find her. I reached out to my sister Lynn in Arizona and together we tracked her down at a local hospital.

Later I found out Ricky's sister Chloe suffered from lupus and was not being properly cared for. I remember hearing Ricky on the phone with his mom discussing his sister moving to California and where she would be able to live. Ricky said, "I'll just move in with Jetaun and she can have my apartment." I could hear Patty say, "Did you talk to Jetaun about this?" and he replied, "She can hear me talking right now," and that is how we moved in together. I didn't know what to say, since he was at my house every day and night anyway. Less than a month later, I helped him pack up his apartment that he once shared with his baby momma. That was something as I found a lot of her stuff that she had left behind, including her high school diploma. It was clear she left in a hurry and did not care what she left or how she left the apartment.

We were now in an undeniable relationship living together. I found myself with a man ten years younger than me, taking care of Jasmine who was around fifteen then, taking care of Da'Sha who was wheelchair bound, still in diapers and G-tube fed, my then six-year-old son, my 10-month-old daughter, and his three-year-old son. Wow . . . and that is where the story of Ricky and Jetaun begins.

Chapter Eight — The Younger Relationship

*A*lthough I was in a new relationship with Rickey, my life with Donald and his family was far from over, because his mom also suffered from substance abuse. Harper, who was living in Atlanta by then, did not think it was in their son's best interest to stay with the grandmother. So, she signed papers for me to care for Jr. The problem was that Jr. did not want to live with me and my new boyfriend; he wanted to be with his grandmother and uncles so they could do whatever they wanted. You see, in my house we have rules, chores, and curfews. But he was a child, and he didn't know what was best for him. So, back and forth to court we went.

Rickey and I fought with Donald's mom to keep custody of his son after he passed away, while Harper was living her best life in another state. It sounds so crazy now. They did not care that he was thriving in school; I had him in counseling to deal with the death of his father and he was on the local baseball team, which he was doing very well in for being his first time playing a sport. Rickey was also into dirt bikes like Donald, so he took him out riding along with his baby momma's little brother, Mikey. Mikey may as well have moved in with us because he and Jr had grown so close being the same age. Yes, I had a house full of kids, but eventually I did not want to fight with Donald's family anymore and realized it was not my battle to fight. His son did not even want to live with me anymore, so why was I fighting so hard? I now understand he would have had a better future with me had he went off to college and played sports or something, instead of living the life he had now.

One day unexpectedly, he showed up at my house. He was all grown up, with long dreads and roughly fifteen chains around his neck. It was obvious he had chosen the same path as his father. We sat in the garage and talked for a while. I expressed my frustrations coming from raising another stepson and the battles we were going through. He expressed himself how he should have stayed here, and he didn't know better at that age. He said nobody bought him a cake or celebrated his birthday since he left my house when he was ten years old. That hit hard and eased my mind greatly, as I thought why I always fought to protect and care for other people's kids.

This relationship with Rickey and I was different from the other relationships I found myself in. Of course, one thing for sure was that he still had a lot more growing to do and still needed to figure out what he wanted to do with his life. He already knew a little something about automobiles, so he enrolled in a few college courses to get his certificate in auto mechanics. I remember being so insecure about him being on campus with all those younger women his age. I was struggling with my emotions and insecurities from all my previous relationships. Don't get me wrong, Rickey had started causing some insecurities in our relationship as well. Yes, I used to track his phone and pop up at the college to spy on him. But this was because I could tell he still had feelings for his son's mom, meaning I didn't believe he was really committed to me. I once found a letter he wrote her from my computer on social media, expressing he still had feelings for her. I also saw her reply to him explaining she didn't want to be with him anymore and had left their son with him because she knew how much he loved him. This was something I couldn't understand as a mother; I could never abandon my child, but this seem to be the type of men I attracted. Harper was the same way.

I remember the first time I met his son's mom, Pam. His son's birthday was approaching, and her mom wanted to buy his son some dirt bike gear. So, we met them at a motorsports store. This man did not know how to handle the situation. Here we were, walking around with Pam and her mom, and he did not even introduce me. I was so angry that I eventually went and sat in the car. When he came out, I cussed him out saying, "How rude, who raised you?" His excuse was that he did not know what to do or how to introduce me. I said, "How about as your girlfriend who you and your son live with?" As if she did not already know from their friends what we had going on. That was that young and dumb frame of mind I had a problem with.

Pam eventually reached out to me on social media when Rickey started keeping their son from her because of the relationships she was in. This was another way I could tell he still had feelings for her, because why else would he care who she was dealing with? At that point I took over visitations, setting up a schedule for her and enforcing it with Rickey. I know sounds crazy, but that was where my mind was. I knew I was a good woman who took care of the home life and kids, but I still wondered what this young man saw in my old ass. Was he just using me? One of his female friends Sarah once told me he was.

Yeah, he had a host of friends from high school that he considered family who hung around all the time. They did not care for me, as I was the controlling lady who did not let Rickey hang out and do whatever he wanted. His male friends were all cheaters, and I did everything in my power to ensure Rickey had no time or opportunity to cheat on me. With technology advancing, I would track his location and pop up on him and his friends. I would chase them down in my truck, bumping them with my truck a few times. Sounds crazy huh? I would go through his phone to see who he was calling and texting. I was definitely acting crazy, and labeled "the crazy lady" by his baby momma Pam. This I know because Camron came home with one of Pam's old phones, and it was still full of text messages between her and all their friends and family, including her new baby daddy. Yeah, I read everything and now knew exactly how everyone really felt about me. You see, they shared the same circle of friends and some family. So, she was there at most of the events and functions we attended. That drove me crazy because I could clearly see that Rickey was not over her and could not understand why she was always included in events where they knew I was coming to. It was like they were trying to start problems or trying to get them back together; I don't know, maybe both. He did not assist in the matter, because he would also say little slick comments and I would catch him looking at her all the time. I have no idea why I did not just walk away from this toxic relationship back then, but something in me would not let this man go. Yes, I saw potential in this man; he was cute, in shape, and was very handy around the house. Jenney loved him, but the unintentional emotional abuse from him and not knowing what he wanted to do was really affecting me.

Regardless of the feelings he still had for Pam, Rickey made a huge decision. Not even a full year into our relationship, Rickey proposed to me on my birthday, and took me away for the weekend. Crazy . . . I remember us having an issue getting the room and his friend Kevin who knew about Rickey's plan to propose giving him the money to pay. I was on the phone with Lynn telling her about the issue and the room when Rickey got on one knee in the hotel room and popped a ring. I quickly told Lynn I would call her back, and of course I said yes. The truth is, I had already seen the ring he hid in Jasmine's closet. Like I said, my insecurities were at an all-time high back then, so nothing was a secret around here. Anyway, now that we were engaged, I started planning my dream wedding. My sister Lynn, Dani, and I would sit on the phone for hours picking colors, venues, caterers, and dresses. I had one-hundred people on my guest list and already started buying decorations, candles, and cake-cutting sets. I was in full-blown wedding mode.

By then I was running my own residential and commercial cleaning company to make some extra money. Jasmine had graduated high school and was about to move in her dorm room for her first year of college. We were so proud of her. Jasmine was like my first child; I raised her, and she helped me to grow. You see, I was young when I got her and had Da'Sha, so those two girls have been rocking with me through all my struggles, tears, fears, and victories. To see her achieving accomplishments were joyful moments. Rickey was also proud of her and helped in any way he could to support her in her new journey as a college kid.

Just like all the other relationships I have had, Rickey and I had had many struggles developing our life together. Who knew we would break up and get back together again and again before we got it right? As an older woman, I knew what I wanted out of a relationship, and I knew what I was not going to accept from a man having learned from my previous relationships. And I made it clear that it was "my way or the highway," and unfortunately it was the highway a few times.

Every time we got into an argument, Rickey would pack up him and Camron and move out. Once, he moved back to his old apartment with his sister. That was dumb because she was young and did not care about our relationship, so she would have gatherings and friends over that Rickey used to be involved with. That did not sit well with me, so I crashed the party a few times and even threw my engagement ring at him like it's over. Another time, he moved to San Jose with his mom and granddad, which was harder because I couldn't just pop in when I wanted to. I found out his mom had gotten him a new phone, so I could not see who he was calling and texting. I assumed he was dealing with other women or even Pam again since they were so fond of her. This was something I could never understand: how his family and friends could still show Pam so much love and respect after abandoning her son and moving on with her life, but disrespect me while I was taking care of Camron like he was my own. For the life of me, I still do not understand it to this day.

Chapter Nine — Life Changing Moment

*I*n November of 2010, my Aunt Jane called to tell me my grandmother had cancer. She said they had known for a while and my grandmother was refusing treatment. She just wanted to be home with her family. Rickey, the kids, and I started making more frequent trips down to Pasadena to see her. She had lost a lot of weight; she was now small-framed and confused at times, but she knew who I was and told me how much she loved me. She also said Rickey was a good man and I should marry him. I still treasure all the pictures we took with her in her last days with my kids, my mom, and Aunt Pauly.

My mom called and said granny was not going to be around much longer, and told me I should get down there. I was struggling to get kids to a sitter and get gas. Unfortunately, my grandmother passed before I could get there. I am grateful that I was able to tell her how much I loved her and thank her for all the years she took care of me. I was handling myself well until the mortuary came to get my grandmother, and I saw her in a body bag. Oh, I lost it. I remember my cousin's boyfriend John catching me as I fell and telling me to breathe, because I was hyperventilating. Someone handed me a paper bag and told me take deep breaths. It took a minute, but I calmed down and gathered myself; this was the exact reason I didn't want my kids to be there. I didn't know how I was going to handle this loss. My granny was my everything.

We all had to pitch in to help pack up my grandmother's apartment. Between all my aunties and uncles, they divided up her belongings. I could tell that the passing of my grandmother took a big toll on my mom. She turned to drugs and alcohol to cope. She now had her own place and Jasmine was living with her when she was not on her college campus. Jasmine was helping her around the house and my mom was helping Jasmine with things she needed for college. I was happy Jasmine was there to help my mom, because it took some of the pressure off of me. I know it may sound selfish, but I was becoming physically and emotionally drained with all the obstacles I had going on in my life.

In 2012, Rickey and I separated again. He moved to North Carolina with Jim and his family to try and get a job. Although we were separated, we still talked on the phone every day for hours. I did not feel at ease, because my insecurities had me thinking it would be easy for him to talk to whoever he wanted out there. My insecurities were at an all-time high. Rickey had said multiple times that we were separated, so he was free to do whatever he wanted. I really did not understand why we were still talking on the phone like we were together. He was keeping me on a string that he could cut at any time. I assumed Jim and Nadine would set him up with someone out there, especially when Nadine had friends over to visit and they were introducing him to new people.

Pam got pregnant with her second kid while Rickey was living in North Carolina with Jim and Nadine. Sidebar: Nadine and Pam are like sisters, so that was an issue in its own. Rickey and Pam had lived with Jim and Nadine before, but decided to return to California when Pam got pregnant with Camron. So, Pam and Nadine had a close relationship unlike me and any of his family members. No matter how nice and helpful I was to them, I never felt genuinely loved: just tolerated. But anyway, I heard about a conversation Rickey had with Pam about her having another baby, as if she were scared to tell him. I could not understand how she was having another kid and didn't take care of Camron. I remember telling Rickey how weird and unsettling that was for me, as I have never had to explain what I had going on with any of my exes. That's how I knew they both probably still had feelings for each other. Instead of letting it go, I put my guard up even more.

That November, Rickey came to visit us for Thanksgiving. I remember it being the first time I ever cooked a whole Thanksgiving meal on my own. I set up a beautiful table presentation with all the food on it, along with desserts. My mom and Rickey were so impressed. Like they say, "A way to a man's heart is through his stomach." Rickey went back to North

Carolina, and we continued talking on the phone every day. He eventually came back to visit in February and decided he wanted to move back. He reached out to his brother, and asked Jim to send the things he left out there by mail.

We worked hard on our relationship over the next couple of years, mainly trying to figure out if it was going to work out or not. We even went to counseling to help with mediating our thoughts and feelings to each other. I'm sure Patty was tired of me calling her to complain about her son. She would tell me how much I reminded her of herself, and I needed to change some of my ways as far as acting controlling. I just felt like she was siding with her son, but appreciated her listening to me vent. Patty and I had gotten in to so many arguments over what they called my "controlling ways." Really, I was just not going to let them treat me any kind of way. I demanded my respect and stood up for myself and kids, which sometimes came off as being harsh and irrational, but when my feelings were hurt my emotions got the best of me, causing violent behavior at times. I was still a good person, just trying to work through my anger issues.

Robert's friend Kevin and his girlfriend Brandi had their first child together: a little boy, and they asked if we would be his godparents. Kevin was one of the friends who did not always care for me, because I did not let Rickey hang out with him. I knew the bullshit he was on. However, they admired us for how well we took care of our children, regardless of our personal issues we were going through. Despite all the fussing and fighting Rickey and I did, people still thought we made great parents and took care of our blended family.

We planned a Valentine's Day weekend in Las Vegas, Nevada with a few other couples. It was Kevin, his girlfriend and baby momma Brandi, Sarah, and Brian. I later found out that Lynn and her family would be in Vegas that weekend as well. It was then in Vegas where we decided to forget the big wedding and just get married right then and there. Rickey and I talked about it that morning in the hotel room and said, "Let's do it." We didn't tell everyone, just Kevin and Brandie, because we were riding together. We had them take us to the hall of records and filed for our marriage license, then found a little hole-in-the-wall wedding chapel. I called Lynn and told her what we were about to do, and she and her family came right over. I remember putting on those rented wedding gowns and my sister asking me, "Are you sure this is what you want to do?" With some doubt in my mind I said, "Yes." Dressed in my wedding dress and Rickey in his tuxedo, we went to swipe the credit card and it got declined. I was like, "Wait there's money in there, try again. Again, it was declined, and I remember Rickey saying that we going to swipe this one more time, and if it does not work it, ain't meant to be. Laughing I said, "Right." Sitting in a chair in a wedding gown, I was waiting to see if this transaction was going to go through. Lynn snapped a picture of me, and I had a look of "whatever" on my face. Rickey swiped the card, and we all held our breath . . . it was approved. The lady said and she called the chaplain to come preform the ceremony. The small crowd of friends and family sat in the small makeshift chapel, and my brother-in-law walked me down the aisle. No one was dressed for the occasion but Rickey and I because it came with our wedding package. Then the chaplain started talking, and it was clear he had a few drinks before he came. He slurred the words and pronounced our names wrong. It was definitely not the wedding of my dreams, but it was done. I look back at our pictures and video, and think to myself that we rushed it. Although I had my best friend and her family there, I felt some type of way. My mom was not there, his mom was not there, and none of our siblings or any of the kids were there. But it was done, so now we had to go celebrate.

We let Rickey's friend Kevin pick the place to celebrate. We rented a limo to drive us around and we ended up at a strip club. What the heck was we doing at a strip club after we just got married? It was a bad idea and a horrible location; the strippers looked like they were starving and needed a meal. They couldn't even dance and when one sat on Rickey's lap, oh no, the attitude came out me. I remember giving him a look and the frail girl got up and walked towards me. She sat next to me and explained she was not trying to be disrespectful. I said, "Don't trip," gave her ass a dollar, and sent her on her way. The attitude was there and noticeable. This was a bad idea, let's go. It was not how I imagined my wedding or wedding night would go.

Back home we showed everyone the video to announce we got married. We got some tears, hugs, backlash, and sarcasm, but we did not care. It was done: we were married and about to start a new journey together as husband and wife.

Not a lot changed in the household after we got married, since we were already functioning like husband and wife in the house as far as duties. I did all the cooking and cleaning, and Rickey did all the outside work. Rickey still didn't have a permanent job and was still looking when he decided he wanted to drive trucks, and needed to get his Class C license to do so. He found a trucking school in Arizona that would train him and put him to work after he completed the course. So, I asked my sister Lynn if Rickey could stay with her for thirty days while he went to this trucking school, and of course she said "yes." For the next thirty days Rickey lived in Arizona, and I stayed in California with our kids. A month or so later my husband had his license to operate a semi-truck. They say blessings happen once you do what's right by God. I feel like us getting married and no longer living in sin opened the doors to greater things and blessings, as we were now one in matrimony in God's eyes.

The checks from Rickey driving trucks were a big help, but the kids and I were missing his presence, and they were starting to act up. You see, by driving trucks Rickey could be gone for weeks at a time, and that was leaving all the responsibilities to me. Taking care of the kids and the house was a lot on me, and I didn't get much help from Rickey's family or friends. I would expect them to help or check on us more with Rickey on the road, but that was not the case. My mom was still coming and going as she liked, but still had her own place and did not care to leave it much now that she was comfortable in her own home. I could not blame her.

Sarah, one of Rickey's female friends, started coming over to hang out with me while Rickey was on the road. She had two kids with one of Rickey's close friends, Brian. Their daughter and Jenny would play together often and became very close. Sarah and her kids came every day while Rickey was on the road. So much so that Rickey started to get irritated, saying Sarah was taking up too much of my time. I think the problem was that he knew Sarah better than me, and he knew toxic ways about her that I had yet to figure out. I am a kindhearted person, and I have always opened my heart and home sometimes to people unworthy of my generosity. I feed kids and plan outings and activities for them. I'm like a mother to everyone's kids, but when things get rough it's only my kids who are left out. When Sarah was doing well, whether it came from a new place to stay, a new relationship, or another friendship in the works, I did not see her much. When she was doing poorly, she was always around. When she got mad, she would not let the girls play with each other, and that was a red flag for me. My daughter used to be so upset and cry because that was her only friend, and this lady was using her kids like pawns in a chess game. I do not like when people put children in the middle of grown folk's issues. Kids have nothing to do with what adults have going on. This was not the first or last time my kids would be affected by an adult's selfish immature actions, as you will hear about later.

One night in December, Rickey and I were hanging out with Kevin and Brandi at our house for my upcoming birthday. We were playing cards and cooking some hot wings when Brian got upset Sarah was ignoring his calls and texts, so he came over and walked right in my house. It was like the devil himself had walked in. He said he was taking the kids because Sarah wasn't dealing with him. Their daughter was crying, and nobody was doing anything. I got in-between Brian and the little girl, and told her to go in my room. I told Brain that he was not about to come in my house and disrespect me or my home, and snatch up the kids out of anger. We yelled at each other for a while before Kevin and Rickey intervened and made him go outside. But he didn't leave, and instead he sat outside my house and busted all the windows and mirrors in Sarah's car. I was so upset that Rickey didn't go outside and address his friends disrespecting our home like that. I called him all kinds of punks because just the night before, we were at his friend's house party and Pam's boyfriend got into it with someone at the party. Rickey was ready to go to war, so I was wondering where all the energy went when it came to protecting his own home. This caused us to get in a big fight and my phone was damaged in the midst of that.

They next day Rickey left with his friends, and I finally plugged the house phone up to find several messages from my little sister Alexus on my dad's side. She said that my little brother Leroy had been shot by the police and died. I was in shock. Sarah called Rickey to come home because she did not want me to drive to Palmdale alone and she was going to stay with my kids. I remember feeling all these emotions on the forty-five minute drive. Rickey was trying to be comforting, but I was still mad at him from the night before. And now I was angry at the police officers who had gunned down my baby brother. I needed answers.

As we pulled up to my sister's house, there were already family and friends there. I remember walking in and going straight to my stepmom and hugging her. I had no words to say; I just wanted to hold her. It was the same with my sisters and brothers; we were all devastated, because he was the youngest of us all. He had two small boys under the age of six years old, and now they were without a father. My stepmom just kept saying, "They killed my baby, the police killed my baby," and then my dad called. We had to tell him his youngest son was killed. The pain I know he felt came from being so helpless. H had now lost his mom, dad, and son while he was locked up. It was two days before my birthday and five days before Christmas.

We would later find out that Leroy had fell asleep in a Taco Bell drive through and hit the side of the building. The workers called the police, saying the driver was unresponsive. However, that is where the story goes sideways. The police had put Leroy in the back of the police car instead of rendering aid and calling an ambulance. They then searched the vehicle, finding a gun and some pills. They claimed this gave them cause for arrest. The officer stated in court that he went to attempt to handcuff Leroy, and he started fighting him. Two other officers attempted to help subdue my brother, one by holding him by the arms and another by holding him on the lower part of his body. The officer states in court that they were beating my brother on his back, and he would not go down. They then heard the third officer say, "Move out the way." When the attorney asked what he interpreted that to mean, the officer said he assumed it meant the third officer was going to shoot his gun. Which in fact he did. That one officer shot my brother nine times, some which were in his back.

I could not for the life of me understand how three officers could not restrain a five-foot, 130-pound guy with a prior back injury from a car accident which cause him to have to wear a back brace. They could not tase him or something? It was like the officer's pride was hurt, so death was the answer. They claimed in court that my brother was high on meth which gave him incredible strength. In our eyes, the police just killed another unarmed black man, and so we marched and rallied for our brother. We screamed "Leroy's Life Matters" all the way to the police station. "No justice, no peace," we yelled with our banners and homemade signs. We made the front-page news, with a picture of his six-year-old son holding a sign that reads "Don't Shoot." My nephew's lives will never be the same. My brother was an excellent father, son, brother, and uncle, and they took that from us in two minutes.

After the death of my little brother, we tried to gather more for holidays as a family. Between my home and Alexus' home, we came together when every we could. We did balloon releases on Leroy's birthday, and the day he was killed in remembrance of his life. Our Christmases have never been the same since the loss of our brother in December of 2015.

Of course, life had to go on for all of us. My husband quit driving trucks so he could be home more. But we also started to have a lot of trust issues with each other, because I had found out that he had been communicating with a woman over the phone while he was on the road. I found this out by looking at the call log from our phone bill. I remember asking, "How dumb do you think I am? Did you think I would not notice a two-hour conversation?" Later I would find out that his little sister Chloe had given him the girl's number. She just showed me that she had no respect for our marriage, and I stopped talking to her for a long time. It took me a long time to get over the fact that Rickey was reaching out to another woman he had been in prior relationships with, and trust was definitely out the door once again. This time it was different because we were married, and I think it hurt my feelings even more.

Eventually, he got a job as a tactical vehicle mechanic at a military base in our area. I started online classes to get my bachelor's degree in business. We also decided to try and have a baby. At that time, I was taking an anti-depressant and knew I had to stop taking it in order to have a baby. Against my counselor's advice, I stopped cold turkey. I said, "I don't need it, I'm going to have a baby." Boy was I wrong. I realized you cannot just stop taking a controlled drug like antidepressants. I was a mess, my mood swings increased, and I would get uncontrollably angry. One time I got so upset at Rickey while we were arguing that I smashed a one-hundred-gallon fish tank with a golf club. That is when I knew I had to get control of my emotions, but it did not stop us from wanting a child together. We found a doctor's office that would perform a tubal reversal. After having my tubes tied for eight or nine years, I could not believe we were about to try to conceive a baby. But we did and for months, then years, we tried to conceive. I went to a specialist to have the flow in my fallopian tubes checked. They told us that one of my tubes was blocked, which limited my chances to conceive in half. You see, women alternate which tube they ovulate on each month. One month we ovulate on the right side, and the next month we ovulate on the left side. Because my right fallopian tube was blocked, it meant I only had a chance of getting pregnant every other month. This was hurtful to find out, but we still wanted to try so we tracked my ovulation days. I took so many pregnancy tests that I lost count and hope. The truth was that I was hurt, and I could not have a baby with my husband. This really affected me emotionally and I could not see it at the time, but trying to conceive a baby and not being able to became depressing. I went from blaming my age to blaming the years of smoking to blaming God. This depression and frustration built up in me for years. I cried every time I took a pregnancy test, and it was negative. Each negative test sunk me deeper into depression.

Trying to find happiness in life, my husband Rickey brought a travel trailer so we could start taking the kids camping. He also purchased a razor, which I call an oversized go kart. So, we started doing family outings where we would camp in the desert and take the kids for rides on the razor and dirt bikes. Even though I was still cooking and cleaning, just in a smaller area, I enjoyed the campfires at night under the stars.

The first camping trip we went on, I invited Pam and her other son with us because it was for Camron's birthday. That was another mistake on my part: trying to be too nice. We had become friends over the years, and I had recently let Pam and her son stay with us for about two weeks at Camron's request, because she was basically homeless at the time. But I was just reminded that my husband was still attracted to Pam; I caught him looking at her as she walked by in her little shorts. I spoke on it saying, "I see you fool I'm not blind or crazy." To this day he denies it, but I know what I saw, and his eyes were definitely on her ass.

The uneasy feeling of being now married to a man who was still in love with another woman was driving me insane. Every time she was around, I would catch Rickey saying some slick comment or staring at her. One day I lost it and launched a glass at Rickey, saying, "What is wrong with you? Do you not see me, your wife, sitting here?" She had said goodbye to a friend and called him Boo. Rickey's response was that I wished my name was Boo. Before I knew it, the glass was in the air. It was so disrespectful to me, and I was not the only one noticing his actions, so I was becoming embarrassed and disrespected. That was it; I cussed Rickey out and made everyone leave. "It's over," I said, once again mad as hell.

A couple of weeks later, I was talking to a couple of women about my issues. One of the women went back and told Pam what I said. Of course, she added details to the story, but whatever she told her caused Pam to never speak to me again. We would be at my stepson's games, and she would walk past me like I did not exist. Pam and this lady would speak to everyone except me. Again, I flashed at Rickey. I told him, "If they don't speak to me, you don't speak to them." The way I saw it was that it was us against the world. But he did not understand that type of energy. He would speak to her and the lady that started the he-said-she-said between us. I would be so upset with him, saying things like, "Pick a side, I'm your wife." Rickey not being able to defend me against the family and friends he knew prior to me was a big issue in our marriage.

The lack of reassurance, protection, and feeling valued was the reason I packed up my whole house and children and moved to Arizona during one of our separation periods. Rickey had already moved out and was living in his travel trailer with Camron, who seemed to be just fine with the arrangements. It gave him and his dad solo time with each other. They went shopping, out to eat, and to the movies quite often while we were separated: things we did not do as a family while we were together.

My kids Da'Sha, Ace, and Jenny and I put our home of seventeen years on the market and moved in with my sister Lynn until we could find a place of our own. That was probably the first mistake. I have been independent and living in my own home since I was twenty years old. I do not know how I thought I could live with my sister, her husband, and their kids. My kids and I were used to having our own space. Now, Da'sha and I were sleeping in their family room behind a curtain. Ace was sharing a room with my one niece, and Jenny was back-and-forth between my younger niece's room and sleeping with me and Da'Sha, because they fought so much. They were both the youngest kids of Lynn and I, so they were spoiled little princesses so that caused conflict. Although Rickey and I were so-called "separated," he was making trips to see us every other weekend. That was a problem for me, because I didn't like him driving on that road like that just to see us. Remember, Donald died on the highway on his way home. So, I worried a lot when Rickey was traveling, especially late nights. In a way, I felt responsible for Donald's death. Remember, I was running away from my problems in Palmdale when I made the move to Adelanto. In the back of my mind and probably the minds of Donald's family, I was the reason he was on the highway that night. Here I was again, running from my problems and moving states. I couldn't be responsible for another life. Wow, I don't think I ever said that out loud before.

Anyway, my sister was working at the time, so that left me at home with Will all day. Will and I got along great, but just sitting at the house with him all day got old. I was bored and smoking a lot to pass the time. Eventually, I got stressed and overwhelmed enough that I called Rickey and told him to come get us. Even though the house was in escrow, I called the trustee and the realtor and told them I was coming back, and I wanted to take the house off the market. Lucky for us, the lawyers had made a mistake on the paperwork, so the sale wasn't final. Of course, Rickey didn't hesitate to come get us. He hitched a ride with his friend Kevin who drove trucks state-to-state and came and got us. We rented a U-Haul, unpacked the storage, and came back to California. My kids were so happy to be back in their own space and so was I. I love my sister to death, but I was making life-altering decisions based on my emotions and not thinking everything through, which is never a good idea.

Rickey and I had a long conversation about what I needed from him as his wife, and he promised he would do his best. I told him I needed protection, reassurance he had my back, that whatever relationship he had with other people could not come before me, and the family foundation we were building together. This caused greater strain on our relationship and sometimes still does. I explained to him that when it comes to his family and friends, he cannot allow any disrespect towards me; it was his job to protect and defend his wife's honor. He has gotten a little better, but I still feel the need to remind him in certain situations.

At the same time, I was still a grown woman and had always been able to stand on my own. So, whether he stood up for me or not, I was going to always defend myself and kids. When his older sister picked up his nieces who were visiting, she told my daughter she couldn't go but she took all the other kids. I wasn't there that day and still thank God, because I do not play about my kids, and I know I would have flipped out for sure. But I was told Rickey said something to his sister about that not being fair, and that he was disappointed in her actions. But I was fueled with so much anger that I banned her from my house, functions, and everything else. I never wanted to see or hear her name again. She had so much audacity excluding my child when I had been so good to all her kids, from babysitting, to helping her clean up and organize her house; and this is how you treat my baby girl. Oh no. She was now dead to me, and I didn't care who didn't like it.

I had been good to her and was very offended by her actions toward my daughter. You see, because Jenny's father died before she was born, she only knew Rickey and his family. The only person from Donald's family who kept in touch after she was born was his sister. Nobody else called or visited. No birthday gifts, no Christmas gifts, nothing; not even Jr. shows her any love. This made me very protective of her and her feelings. I have always felt Rickey's family treated my kids different from Camron, and I let things slide for a long time, but now I was over it. Unlike Camron, Jenny didn't have another side of the family to buy things and show love. Camron had his dad's family, his mom's family, me, and my family. My family and I have always showed Camron the same love as all the other kids, including him in everything. Hell, I threw him his first real birthday party because Sarah told me he never had one; I went all out with that Lego themed party. It was definitely one of the coolest parties I threw. I was sure to do whatever Cameron's mom didn't do; she missed birthdays, I did extra, she couldn't do Christmas, I had it covered. Camron had aunties, uncles, two set of grandmas, and two sets of grandpas. My kids didn't have all that, so they relied on me and Rickey. Ace did have family on his dad's side, but Jenney nor Da'Sha had any so hurting my girl's feelings was intolerable. I didn't care who it was.

Of course, I've always been very protective of Da'Sha and her health. We hadn't heard from D-Mack in years. The last time I reached out to him I was living in Palmdale, and he was married to his high school sweetheart from Pasadena; they were living in Hawaii with his dad. When I called, he asked how I got his number and made it very clear he wanted nothing to do with Da'Sha, so I left him alone. One day, I got a letter from Child Support saying they kept a check he sent. Da'Sha had not been on the county in over ten years, so I took him to court for child support. Da'Sha was eighteen by then, but California child support law states that if a child is disabled, both parents are still responsible for the child. Anyway, going to court didn't go too far. The judge ordered him to pay $125.00 a month, which he did for the first few months, then it stopped. At court he never asked how she was doing or requested to see her, so I said, "Fuck him." I am not begging anyone to be a part of my child's life. Well, during one of our stays in the hospital I made a social media post asking for thoughts and prayers for Da'Sha. Well, it got back to D-Mack, and he reached out. He said he wanted to see her and possibly be a part of her life. He was now married to another woman and had children with his new wife. I think that made six kids for him then. I asked how he got my number, and he said he found it on the child support papers from years earlier. Showing no ill feelings, I let him, his new wife, and kids come see Da'Sha. She sat next to that man like she knew that was her dad with a huge smile on her face.

After several visits they asked if Da'Sha could spend the weekend with them. They said they would have his cousin Tay with them who was very familiar with Da'Sha and all her needs, so I allowed the visit. This arrangement went on for about a year; they would come visit and took Da'Sha for the weekend a few times. This was a blessing to me, as I never got time off caring for Da'Sha. Rickey and I went on a couple of getaways together without kids, and it was nice. The following year I threw Da'Sha a birthday party and they came to celebrate with us. I am big on parties and always have a theme for every party I throw. This party was a *Breakfast at Tiffany's* themed party. We had a brunch-style menu, set up with waffles, chicken, bacon, potatoes, eggs, and more. We dressed up in pretty black dresses and had diamonds and pearls everywhere. The pictures came out so cute and Da'Sha was all smiles.

Shortly after that, the phones calls and visits just stopped. Later, I got a big box in the mail: it was full of stuff Da'Sha had left at their house along with a late birthday gift they had missed. Needless to say, that situation lasted about a year. Then one day I was surfing the internet and saw D-Mack had just brought a new house and had a BBQ to celebrate. I went off and blasted him for being a dead-beat dad all over social media. Why would you send my baby's stuff back in a box like she was no longer welcome at your house? I have not heard from them since, and the child support checks stopped too. Now the checks come every so often, like they send it when they feel like it. I left that whole situation alone because God don't like ugly, and he will get what's coming to him for not showing Da'Sha the love she deserved. I really do not understand or have respect for these parents who decide they can be a parent at their convenience.

Chapter Ten — Stuck In The Shed

needed a place where I could have "me time" away from the kids and husband. So, Rickey brought me a shed that we call my "She Shed," where I can hang out with my friends or alone, and have time to myself to do homework or event projects I would work on for parties. The shed was delivered and placed in the backyard, and over time we had drywall installed and painted the walls. I added some shelves, a futon, and a tv and it was like my own tiny home (without a bathroom of course). It was a great space to chill with friends and family when they came to visit. It was only for adults; I had a small bar and hookah set up, so no kids were ever allowed in the shed.

I found myself in the shed more then I was in the house. I would get up, get the kids off to school, feed and change Da'Sha, then off to my shed I would go. Staying out there, I watched Da'Sha on the camera while I was watching TV, talked on the phone while I smoked pot, or complete homework. Sometimes I was doing all at the same time. I'd have the TV on while smoking a blunt on the phone and doing homework. I was working on my degree and creating LLC's for our family-owned businesses. I created an LLC for a trucking company for Rickey as a birthday gift, because it was something he always talked about. Talk about multitasking; I had it down to a science.

This comfort space started to become a toxic gateway. I started going to the shed to smoke more and more often. I smoked to clean the house, I smoked to cook a meal. If I was upset, I'd go smoke. If I was sad or depressed, I would go smoke. If I had company, we were definitely going to smoke. I was smoking to cope with all aspects of my life, and it was starting to affect my world. I wasn't spending much time with my kids as I used to. I didn't care to be bothered with Rickey at all. Let me tell you, they were the stress in my life. All my years of taking care of kids and adults and never really living my life for myself was now taking a toll on me. I was stressed and depressed, and weed was a way to numb the pain.

Then Covid hit. Rickey got it first, and he had all the symptoms: fatigue, body aches, breathing issues and all. This was cause for all of us to get tested. Rickey and Camron came back positive, so they needed to be quarantined. Rickey went to the travel trailer and Camron stayed in his room. This went on for about a week. Camron only had a headache and tested negative after the first week, but Rickey was in the travel trailer thinking he was going to die because his symptoms were so bad. I remember him telling us how much he loved us through a text message, because he didn't feel like he was going to survive. Wearing gloves and a mask I had to take care of everybody, delivering food and meds to everyone's room and disinfecting the house every day to ensure the germs didn't spread through the house. With Da'Sha having health issues, breathing issues being one of them, it was very important that I didn't spread anything to her. Rickey finally started to get better but was prescribed an inhaler to help his breathing. He still suffers from breathing issues due to Covid. Because the kids were in school, and Rickey was working at the military base, Rickey, Da'Sha, and I decided to get the Covid vaccination to help reduce the chances of us contacting the virus. Because the vaccination was so new, we decided not to get the younger kids vaccinated. Jenny would contract the virus months later along with Rickey again, but this time Rickey was vaccinated and had less symptoms. This time I sent Ace and Camron to stay with family until the house was cleared of the virus. I still thank God Da'Sha and I have never tested positive, even though I had to care for a house full of covid patients several times.

Chapter Eleven: Unexpected Blessing

One day I was in my shed and Ace came in, and I could tell something was wrong. He said, "Mom, I need to tell you something." He was holding his cell phone in his hand, and I glanced down at it. I saw a picture of a home pregnancy test. I just shook my head and told him to get out. Then I proceeded to ask why. I knew him and his girlfriend were having sex so we gave him condoms, because kids are going to do what they want anyway, and I wanted to protect him as best as I could. I thought we had talked to him enough for him to understand the consequences. I guess not, because now he had a baby on the way. I was so disappointed, because I wanted him to go to college like Jasmine did and find a career before starting a family. But like they say, if you want to make God laugh, tell him your plan.

April of 2021, we threw a gender reveal for him and his now baby momma Brittney. It was a successful event. The theme was Lilo (blue) and Angel (pink) and as always, I did all the decorations. We were all over the shock of Ace having a baby so young, but excited for the new arrival. Rickey and I had come to the conclusion that this was the baby we couldn't have, and we would love and spoil her forever.

That June, Ace graduated high school. I threw him a graduation party and eighteenth birthday party in one a day before he turned eighteen years old. With everyone in attendance he didn't seem to be happy, because I think he was expecting a new car or something. The next day, he turned eighteen and moved in with his girlfriend Brittney and her parents. He had been trying to stay over there for a long time and I wouldn't allow it because he was underage, but when I say they couldn't wait to play house, they couldn't wait. The blessing is that her parents love my son and always have the brag on how respectful he is and what a hard-working and good father he is. So, I'm comfortable with him living there, but boy was it hard at first. I was no longer comforted by walking past his room knowing he was safe. Now I had to track his phone in the middle of the night to ensure he made it home safe from work. These kids have no idea how a mother stresses over them.

It was July First, and Rickey and I finally decided to buy Ace a new car as a late graduation and eighteenth birthday gift. While at the dealership we looked at a few cars, but God kept telling me a small SUV, even though I knew he would prefer the Honda Accord. I listened to my gut, and we got him a Nissan Rouge SUV. We dropped it off to him at his job and took the old Impala back. He was so happy, and it was right on time now that he was about to be a father.

Two weeks later, my daughter Jenny had a praise dance performance at another church down the hill. Kevin's mom Mary rode with me, as we had become close while I was entering a spiritual awakening. At church I found myself praying hard for Ace. Mary said I talked about him the whole time in the car, as if he was weighing on my spirit. That night as I settled in for bed, my phone rang, and it was Ace. He said, "Mom I got hit." All I asked was, "Where are you at?" as I slipped on my shoes and woke up Rickey.

Staying on the phone with Ace I asked him if he was OK, and he said yes, because he was able to get out of the car, but his knee and head were hurt. In tears, not knowing what to expect, Rickey flew through traffic and red lights getting there. When we pulled up all we saw were flares and four cars in the middle of the road. My son's SUV was completely totaled; he was hit head-on by one car, which spun him around. Then, he was hit by a second car. "Oh my God" was all I could say through tears, checking on my son and his minor injuries. I thanked God for protecting my son. This was why I kept hearing "SUV" in my head at the dealership. A little Honda would have never been able to sustain the double impact that the SUV took. That SUV saved my son's life that night, and God made sure of that. Brittney and I went to the hospital with him, and her dad and Rickey stayed behind to deal with the police and tow company.

My son was the only one injured in that four-car accident. The lady who caused it said she looked up and couldn't stop, so to avoid hitting the car stopped in front of her, she swerved into oncoming traffic and hit my son. This was on a two-lane highway that has taken multiple lives. What she was doing that had her distracted while driving, we don't know, but God had them all covered that night. Since Ace was injured, I convinced him and Brittney to stay with us until he healed. I was grateful that they agreed. Watching my son in pain at night and on crutches broke my heart, but I know from experience how bad it could have been, so I was grateful. They ended up staying for about three weeks and then returned to her parents' house. I couldn't wait to get to church and tell them my son's testimony. I knew God had been guiding me through all my decisions so he could protect my son's life.

12 days of Hospice

Early September Jasmine called and said they found my mom unresponsive on the floor in her apartment. This was not the first time someone had found my mom unresponsive in her apartment. She had been taking prescription medication irresponsibly for years and drinking alcohol. They took her to the hospital, and she was breathing but not coherent. They said they would keep her for observation and keep us posted. This had become a routine with my mom where she would take too many pills and lose a few days, but in this case, they think she may have had a stroke.

My mom slept for seven days in that hospital. On a Sunday morning I got a phone call, and it was my mom saying "Taun!" I was so happy that I jumped up and got dressed for church. I couldn't wait to tell everyone who had been praying for my mom that she had woke up. It was at that service we had a guest speaker, and the lady pastor picked me out of the audience, saying she would give me a new heart. I stood there with my eyes closed, head bowed, and arms outstretched, hearing her say God wants to give someone a new heart. She said the heart had been broken and abused, and God wanted to give them a new one. The pastor said, "I can't tell what her shirt says but it's her." Mary was standing next to me and gave me a little shove and said, "She's pointing at you." I looked up and the pastor said, "Yes you, come up here." My shirt said "#OnGod." I went up to the altar and received my new heart. I left church feeling so blessed and thankful.

After church I went down to see my mom, and I could tell she was still not completely well. She couldn't remember things and was confused, and she couldn't walk because her legs were so swollen. The doctors said it was because of the stroke, and they needed to do more tests on her. She stayed in the hospital another two weeks. They wanted to do physical therapy, but she said it hurt too much and refused to participate. This caused the hospital to send her to another facility. When I went to see her, the place smelled of urine and was full of old people. My mom said the nurses were mean and not taking care of her. I instantly thought they put my mom in here to rot and die. After I cussed every nurse in that place out, I called the doctor from the parking lot and requested he move her to a hospital, not a convalescent home. I waited in the parking lot until transportation came to get my mom and take her to another hospital. Because of Covid there were a lot of protocols and restrictions at the hospitals which made it difficult for visitors, but I was going to make sure my mom was moved that day. They moved her to a hospital we were familiar with, and the nurses were familiar with her which gave us some relief.

On September 25th, my beautiful, healthy granddaughter was born. We all fell in love with her; it was like she brought sunshine into our dark lives. Comforted that my mom was in a hospital being taken care of, Rickey and I took the kids to Arkansas to Lynn's oldest daughter's wedding. Yes, these kids were growing up, getting married and having babies. The wedding was beautiful, but I got a phone call on our way home from the nurses at the hospital. My mom was refusing therapy again, and they wanted to send her somewhere else. I told them to wait until I got there so I could talk to her, and possibly convince her to participate in the physical therapy they wanted her to do.

This would go on for another month from one hospital to another. My mom had been transferred from multiple hospitals since she was found on her apartment floor in September. It was now November, and we were at the last hospital. The doctor told us bluntly that my mom was dying and there was nothing they could do. He said she had cirrhosis of the liver, her kidneys were failing, and she had a blood clot in her heart that could burst at any time. I wondered why no other hospital had told us she was dying; I was shocked and confused. He said we can keep her here and keep her comfortable or she could go home on hospice. There was no compassion in his voice. This made me think back to one day I was leaving my mom's apartment. I had taken my mom grocery shopping and I was leaving her building when I had a thought in my head (or heard a voice in my head, I didn't know at the time), but it said that my mom was not going to be with us much longer. I remember crying so hard in her parking lot and not completely understanding what I was feeling then. Now I know it was God preparing me again for what was to come.

It was just me and my mom there; my mom just screamed and cried out, "I'm dying, I'm dying" as I held her. I called Jasmine, who was getting ready to go to Vegas for her thirtieth birthday, and told her she needed to come to the hospital. When she got there, I had to tell her our mom was dying, and it broke her; the look in her eyes broke my heart. All those years of protecting her, and this was something I couldn't protect her from, it was out of my control. I told her to go and try to enjoy her birthday, and I would handle this until she came back. I called my husband and my aunts and told them what was going on. My husband said to bring her home. I didn't know how I was going to get through this, but I knew I had to do it, so I started making plans to take my mom home with me on hospice.

Before I left the hospital, Rickey had cleared out Ace's room and the hospice company had already delivered a hospital bed and supplies. It was a little after 12a.m. when the ambulance pulled up with my mom. I opened the front double doors of our house and said, "Welcome home mom." She replied "Hi Taun" as the transport team wheeled her into Ace's room and put her in the hospital bed that was delivered. A few hours later the first hospice nurse came by to check on us. He gave me a bag of just in case medication and a bag of as-scheduled medication; most of it was for pain and to keep her comfortable. Her body was sore to the touch, and we couldn't hold her hand or change her without her screaming in pain. The first night I was alone with her just watching her sleep. The second night my mom's best friend came to stay and by the third night my Aunt Pauly was there, so I was never totally alone in the caring of my mom.

The nurses that came were very nice and comforting. They helped wash her and keep her clean. The hospice company provided all the necessary supplies like an oxygen machine, nebulizer, and suction machines. I was familiar with all the equipment because I used the same type with Da'Sha. They also provided a handbook that described the events that were going to take place during this transitioning of my mom. This book helped me to understand and know what to be prepared for. While reading this little blue book I realized my mom had already begun the transitioning phase at the hospital and we didn't know. According to the book, my mom was in the last two weeks of her life.

I opened my home to all family and friends who wanted to come and say their goodbyes. I played gospel everyday all day, keeping peace and the holy spirit in the house. My mom had visitors every day: family I hadn't seen or spoke with in years came to say goodbye, tell stories, and pray with and for my mom and my household. They brought food, flowers, cards, and money.

The hardest part was seeing my son come by every day to see his granny like that. They were so close; she was his best friend. They truly loved each other and talked on the phone all the time. This was breaking my son's heart, and I couldn't fix it. Jasmine was coming up to visit as well but was not handling things well at all. Here I was again, forced to hide my pain to be strong for everyone else. I went to the bathroom and cried by myself, so my family didn't see me breaking down. My son Camron caught me once and said, "Mom why are you crying?" with a devastated look in his eyes. He looked so lost, like he had never seen mom cry. It was then he knew something was wrong. He had just lost his grandma on Pam's side a couple years before in November as well.

The days were passing, and my mom had stopped eating and drinking. I was constantly checking her oxygen level and heart rate with a pulse ox monitor I had for Da'Sha. I gave her medication needed to keep her comfortable, and then she would start making a gurgling noise as if she was drowning. I would suction her mouth thinking it would help her. I later found out it's called the death gurgle. The reality was that it was part of the process of her body shutting down. I would just cry as I was suctioning her, because I knew it wasn't helping her but me nor my Auntie could bear to listen to the gurgling noise and not do something. So, all throughout the day I cried and suctioned my mom because it was all I could do.

As the days went by, I knew it was getting closer to her passing, so I told my kids to say their goodbyes. It was November 16th, 2022, and I reached out to the mortuary to set up arrangements and made a few calls to family. I took a nap on the couch where I had been sleeping since my mom arrived. When I woke up to check my mom's vitals, her oxygen levels and heart rate were extremely low. I called my sister and told her she needed to come up as soon as possible, because I didn't think mom was going to last much longer. She said that she was on her way. I also called my husband and told him that he should probably come home too. My godsister Dani and cousin sat in the shed waiting on me to come out to smoke, but something told me to sit with my mom. As I set with her, I watched her vitals drop. I held her hand and told her it was fine for her to rest now. I told her not to worry about the kids, I've got the kids, and that I loved her very much. I watched her take her final breath, and then my Aunt Pauly walked in. I said, "She's gone," and broke down in my aunt's arms. My mom was gone.

I texted my cousin in the shed that she was gone, and her and Dani came running. They found me outside, trying to keep my emotions together. I had to call my sister and tell her our mom had passed. Oh my God, the scream she let out haunts me. I couldn't do anything but listen and cry. She made me promise not to let them take her mom before she got there. Then I had to send my son's girlfriend and her mom to get Ace from work, because I knew he wasn't going to take it well and I didn't want him to drive. I called my other siblings, and they were on their way. I knew I needed my family for strength.

The mortuary sent transportation for my mom within the hour. I asked if they would wait for Jasmine to get here before they removed her, as I promised my sister I would. When my sister got there, I knew she was going to get weak in the knees and drop, so I prepared myself to catch her. As we walked to the room, where our mom laid, I stood behind my sister with my arms under her arms as we reached the doorway; I felt her weight drop. I braced myself and I just held her and said, "I got you baby." I have always had her back, and as I told my mom, I always would. When it was time for the mortuary to wheel my mom out in that black body bag, I sent Ace and Jasmine down the street. I remember what that scene did to me when my grandmother passed, and I needed to protect them from as much traumatic damage as I could. As if losing their mom and grandmother wasn't bad enough, I couldn't bear them having those flashbacks in their heads.

My Aunt Pauly never left my side; she stayed with me the entire twelve days my mom was on hospice. She was on the phone with other family members making notifications to everyone who had been a part of my mom's final days. I recall my aunt handing me the phone for one of my older cousins and she just kept saying, "Well done Jetaun." Later I would find out that "Well done" is what God says to his good and faithful servants (Matt.25:21). In my eyes I wasn't doing enough, because I couldn't save my mom's life or save my kids from the heartache. But to my family, I had done what was needed of me in God's eyes. Now I had to prepare to bury my mom.

Although my mom had life insurance, it wasn't enough to cover the cost of the funeral service and expenses. My godsister set up a Go Fund me on social media and a few family members and friends made donations, but the bulk of the cost I took responsibility for, and I had to get a loan which I am still paying back to this day. We knew our mom wanted to be buried with her mom, who also passed in November ten years ago prior. Here I went again, making funeral arrangements for someone I love while trying to be strong for everyone else. Back to the shed I went.

With my mom gone, holidays have not been the same. Jasmine and I talk more, and her hugs are longer and stronger. My son was depressed and angry, and as for me, I'm just here. I know my mom and I had a dysfunctional relationship, but the love was strong. I wish we had more time together, and I cry every time I think about her never getting to hold her great granddaughter. In some ways it takes me back to the pain of Donald passing, never getting to hold our daughter. I wish we had gotten the correct diagnosis before it was too late. Bouncing her from hospital-to-hospital when she should have been home with her family, at least she would have been able to spend more time with us while she was alert and talking. In some ways, I blame myself for not understanding the situation better. I thought it was like all the other hospital visits and she would be okay, but I blamed myself for not acting sooner to bring her home.

Then one day I got a phone call from my cousin, who was a licensed psychiatrist. She said she had a message from my mom. At first I was confused, but she said that my mom sent her to me because she knew I trusted her and would believe what she had to say. She went on to tell me that she belongs to a group of mediums, and during a recent meeting my mom showed up. She told her to call me and let me know that she loved me, and she wanted me to be happy. My cousin and I sat on the phone for almost two hours talking about my mom, my life, her life, and more. I cried like a baby but felt better after that phone call.

Changing My Life

It's May 2022 and I had a tooth ache that had been bothering me for a while, and my jaw was swollen. I looked like the elephant woman. I decided I should go to the emergency room to get checked out. I was not there for an hour, and they said I had an abscess and needed to be admitted for treatment. I panicked. I had never been admitted to the hospital for anything other than having a baby. I called Rickey, told him what was going on, and said he needed to come get my car because they were transporting me by ambulance to another hospital better equipped to handle my care.

I had ridden in plenty of ambulances with Da'Sha, but never with me as the patient. On top of that, the hospital they were transferring me to was almost two hours away in Palm Springs. Hooked up to monitors, I felt all my mom's anxiety when she was in the hospital. Rickey came down to see me and brought some necessities, along with my laptop so I could keep up with my schoolwork. But this was hard for me, because I had never been down like this and went through a lot of emotions in the hospital.

I started detoxing from the marijuana, so I was nauseous and suffering from headaches and chills. I was honest with the nurses that I was detoxing, and they asked the doctor to prescribe something for the nausea which did help. However, I started having panic attacks. My anxiety was starting to get the best of me; I had a full meltdown when they tried to do a CT scan of my face. Laying on that table in that machine for twenty to thirty minutes had me hyperventilating. The nurse had to stop the scan and gave me some medication to calm me down. It was in the hospital I decided to take that opportunity to stop smoking weed. I realized that all the smoking had not just numbed the pain and depression I was feeling from life but subdued other health issues from me that needed to be addressed. God told me it was time for a change, and I needed to take better care of myself. Otherwise, I would not be able to take care of my family, and it had to start with me and my health.

When I got released from the hospital, I told Rickey about my decision to stop smoking. I explained to him that it was going to be hard in the beginning and I was going to need his full support. He agreed he would help however he could, and told me how proud he was of me for making that decision on my own. Lord, I didn't know how detoxing from marijuana was going to affect me physically and emotionally. I went into full depressed mode. I didn't want to talk to anyone, I didn't want visitors, and was not replying to text messages. I did nothing but lay in my bed in a dark room and watched TV. I didn't know at the time, but Lynn and Dani were corresponding with each other about getting a psychiatrist for me and reaching out to Rickey to get insurance information on doctors. Dani and Lynn, both made me promise to reply at least once a day, so they knew I was okay. Dani had texted and wanted to come get Da'Sha so I could rest, and I remember replying rudely, "No, I can take care of my own baby." It was bad. I was fussing at Rickey for not tending to my emotional needs, and even told him I wanted a divorce because he did not know how to love me how I needed to be loved. I was a wreck and pushing everyone away. Brittney reached out to me about Ace and his anger issues, and I told her she was going to have to figure it out because I could not even help myself. I felt so bad not being able to be there for my kids, but I was going through a mental breakdown and could not help anyone during that time. All I could do was lay in bed and cry.

Ace had not taken the news of me being in the hospital well. He and his little family were vacationing at a cabin in Big Bear, California and when Brittney's mom told him I was in the hospital, he got upset. He did not pay attention, tripping over a gate and fracturing his elbow. They had to take him to the hospital, and he was placed in a cast. He was not used to his mom being down or unavailable. My kids looked at me like I'm Wonder Woman, never sick or hurt, always there for them. He had just lost his granny and did not know what to do with his mom in the hospital.

I knew it was time to snap out of this state of mind, so I pushed myself out of bed. I started cleaning my house and cooking meals for my family. I went to church and the pastor prayed for me, along with Mary. I had grown very close to her, and she had basically taken me under her wing since I started my spiritual awakening journey and the loss of my mom. She taught me how to hear when God is speaking to me and how to learn to control my emotions. I started to feel like myself again physically. But mentally, I was a still a wreck. I had been numbing my thoughts and pain for so long with the weed that when I stopped, it all hit me like a ton of bricks. The issues between my husband and I, loss of my mom, the struggle of taking care of a disabled child, and so much more took a toll on me. I laid in that bed and cried for the whole two weeks. But when I came out of that room, I was stronger than ever. I had an appetite, I was able to sleep, and most of all, I had a clear mind. That self-imposed detox was well overdue and now I had to revamp my life.

Then one day I was scrolling on social media and ran across an ad on getting help with writing a book. I had already thought about writing children's books about Da'Sha and the different scenarios we have come across in our life. But when I talked to the publisher, we decided I should first work on my memoir, which is where this book began.

About a month later I started suffering from major migraines. For days I could not sleep, with my head pounding. I finally went to the doctor to find out I had high blood pressure which was causing the migraines. Not being a fan of medication, I went home to see if I could try some home remedies. That did not work; my blood pressure was 145/110 and not going down. I eventually went back to the doctor so she could prescribe a low dose of blood pressure medication. After a day of taking the medication, my head felt better, and my blood pressure was back to normal. I thought it was so crazy how I now had all these medical issues after I stopped smoking weed. But I guess the marijuana was subsiding the symptoms of these issues I was having as I grew older.

Da'Sha is now twenty-six years old and doing well. She has learned how to communicate with me through her Leapfrog and Fisher price plush toys which all say different phrases such as, "I love you," "Can I have a snack please," and "I love to cuddle." They also sing her melodies and teach her alphabets and counting. She still suffers from seizures from time to time. Her seizures range from mild twitches to full blown grandma seizures, so if we are not paying close attention to her, we can miss her having a mild seizure and she can stop breathing. She still requires 24-hour care and supervision. Jenny is about to start her first year of high school and is excited to try out for the cheer squad and the volleyball team. Camron is going starting 11th grade and preparing to go to the Air Force. Ace is still living with Brittney, and her parents, Brittney, and him are both working on their medical degrees. Rickey and I are proud to be owners of multiple businesses and are enjoying our beautiful granddaughter. We are teaching our children the importance of having proper education, good credit, and investing their money and owning property. This will help them to be successful, and hopefully debt free, leading them to financial wealth as adults. These are important aspects of life we were not taught as children and had to figure it out on our own the hard way.

My life has not been easy and there has been a lot of heartache and pain, but there has also been some blessings, joys, and victories. All of which has made this Capricorn stronger and thankful for the woman I am working to become a great mother, wife, grandmother, sister, and friend. I am no longer that insecure little girl hurt by her past relationships and issues. I have learned from my mistakes and take pride in my growth. I am comfortable in my skin and thankful for trials and tribulation that help me to grow. My story is not finished. It is still being written, and I am excited to see what else God has in store for my life. So, let's end this book with "To be continued." Until next time, be blessed.

Made in the USA
Columbia, SC
08 July 2024

38302870R00072